YUGOSLAVIA IN TURMOIL

YUGOSLAVIA IN TURMOIL:
after self-management?

Edited by
James Simmie and Jože Dekleva

Pinter Publishers
London and New York

First published in Great Britain in 1991 by
Pinter Publishers Limited
25 Floral Street, London WC2E 9DS

British Library Cataloguing in Publication Data

A CIP catalogue record for this book is available from the
British Library
ISBN 0 86187 141 3

Library of Congress Cataloging-in-Publication Data

Yugoslavia in turmoil: after self-management?/[edited by] James
    Simmie and Jože Dekleva.
        p.   cm.
    Includes bibliographical references and index.
    ISBN 0-86187-141-3
    1. Yugoslavia—Economic policy—1945–   2. Yugoslavia—Social
policy.   3. Yugoslavia—Politics and government—1980–   I. Simmie,
James.   II. Dekleva, Joze.
HC407.Y824   1991
338.9497—dc20   91-22151
                                                                        CIP

Typeset by BookEns Limited, Baldock, Herts.
Printed and bound in Great Britain by Biddles Ltd of Guildford and Kings Lynn

CONTENTS

LIST OF CONTRIBUTORS

Ognjen Čaldarović is full professor of sociology at the Faculty of Philosophy, Department of Sociology, University of Zagreb. His publications on urban sociology include: *Social theory and the urban question* (1985), *Contemporary society and urbanisation* (1987), *Social fragmentation of space* (1989) and *Energy and society* (forthcoming).

Barbara Verlič Dekleva is a graduate student of the University of California and received her PhD at the University of Zagreb. Since 1974 she has been a research member of the Institute for Sociology in Ljubljana. Her field of work and publications concern urban sociology, particularly urban renewal, housing, social policy and quality of life.

Jože Dekleva completed undergraduate studies, and later taught at the University Institute for Architecture in Venice. His graduate studies were at University of California, Los Angeles. He is director of Urban Planning at the Institute of Slovenia, Yugoslavia and was previously a research fellow at the same Institute. At OECD he is the Yugoslav delegate covering the areas of urban problems.

Pavel Gantar obtained his MA in Political Sciences in 1983 from the University of Ljubljana, Yugoslavia. He is at the University of Ljubljana, in the Faculty of Sociology, Political Sciences and Journalism, and as an assistant teacher has been involved with teaching courses on sociology of local communities and urban sociology and planning.

Zagorka Golubović is Full Professor at the Faculty of Philosophy, University of Belgrade where she graduated in philosophy in 1952. From 1957–75 she was an assistant, then Associate Professor at the University of Belgrade before being dismissed for political reasons. In 1981 she was given a new post at the University as a Research Fellow in the Institute for Social Sciences. She is a member of the Council of International Sociological Association.

Bogomir Kovač is Assistant Professor at the Faculty of Economics, University of Jubljana, Yugoslavia. His publications include *Socialism and*

Market Economy (1982), *Political Economy of Capitalism and Socialism* (1986), *Mode of Production and Critical Political Economics* (1988).

Srna Mandič, Institute for Sociology, University of Ljubljana, Yugoslavia. She was appointed as Research Officer at the Institute for Sociology in 1984 and has been a principal researcher on a number of research projects on the Yugoslav system of housing policy and its transformations. She is currently involved in research on non-profit housing and is one of the founding members of a promotion agency for non-profit housing in Ljubljana.

Tomaž Mastnak has a degree in sociology, MA in philosophy and PhD in social sciences. He is currently working at the Institute of Philosophy in the Centre of Scientific Research at the Slovene Academy of Sciences and Arts as a Senior Research Fellow. He has published books and essays on Stalinism and democratic opposition in Eastern Europe.

Jože Mencinger is Professor of Economics at the University of Ljubljana, Yugoslavia and since 1990 is vice-prime minister with the Slovenian government. He is associated with the Economic Institute of the Law School, the leading institution in econometric research. He has been a visiting professor with the universities of Maribor, Zagreb and Pittsburgh. He is a consultant with the World Bank. His writings have included the Yugoslav economic system and most of its econometric models and he has contributed to a number of international conferences.

James Simmie is a reader in Planning and Sociology in the Planning and Development Research Centre at the Bartlett School of Planning, University College, London. He teaches courses on planning and sociology, and post-industrial society and the future of cities. His research interests include the sociology of city planning, international comparative planning in capitalist, mixed and socialist economies and the significance of new technologies for the future of systems of post-industrial cities. He has written extensively on these subjects. His main publications include *The Sociology of Internal Migration* (London, Centre for Environmental Studies, 1972), 'Physical planning and social policy' in R. Raynor, and J. Haden (eds), *Cities, Communities and the Young* (London, Routledge and Kegan Paul, 1973), *Citizens in Conflict: a sociology of town planning*, (London, Hutchinson, 1974), *Power, Property and Corporatism; the political sociology of planning* (London, Macmillan, 1981), 'Corporatism and planning' in W. Grant, ed. *The Political Economy of Corporation*, (London, Macmillan, 1985), with S. French, *Corporatism, Participation and Planning: the case of contemporary London* (Oxford, Pergamon, 1989) and with R. King, *The State in Action: public policy and politics*, London, Pinter. He is currently working on an international comparative study of the results and outcomes of planning in California, Britain and Slovenia.

Janez Šmidovnik is councillor of the Legislation Service of the government of the Republic of Slovenia, where he deals with organisational problems of public administration and local government. He is professor at the Administrative School in Ljubljana, Yugoslavia and lectures on the theoretical basis of management and administration. At the Faculty for Sociology and Political Sciences he conducts the post-graduate education for public administration. His publications include *Yugoslav Commune Conception* (1970), *Basic Administration Conceptions* (1980), *Theoretical Management and Administration Basis* (1985).

LIST OF TABLES

FOREWORD
PROGRAMME OF REFORMS IN YUGOSLAVIA

It must be admitted that it has taken Yugoslavia some time to face up to the crisis it entered in the 1980s. Currently, inertia of another kind prevails in Yugoslavia and in the world. Owing to the fact that the political turmoil in the country, which has captured the fascinated attention of both journalists and the public, the world seems to be unaware that in 1989 and at the beginning of 1990 the new Yugoslav government, headed by Ante Marković, embarked upon a radical reform which will rapidly enable Yugoslavia to join the ranks of free market democracies.

1. Approach to the reform

When the present Yugoslav Government assumed office on 16 March 1989 it announced *three key reform targets*: first, the establishment of integrated markets in goods and services, capital and labour; second, the opening-up of the country to the world, i.e. the internationalization of the national economy and culture, and third, the strengthening of the legal system, including the expansion of human rights.

In view of its constitutional role according to the constitution, the government had to put the emphasis on the economic system and economic trends where the gravest problems were concentrated. These problems spread to other areas so that it can be said that the roots of the Yugoslav economic, political and even moral crises lie in the economic sphere. Once the economic issues are resolved, it will be easier to find more productive and efficient solutions to the other problems facing Yugoslavia.

2. Changes in the economic system

The government proposed a number of laws which were adopted by the Assembly of Yugoslavia, including the following: Enterprises; Co-operatives; Banks and Other Financial Institutions; the National Bank of Yugoslavia; Labour Relationships; Foreign Trade, Foreign Exchange Transactions; Free Trade and Duty Free Zones, Securities, the Money Market and the Capital Market; Social Capital; and Foreign Investments.

The main characteristic common to all these laws is *property pluralism*. All types of ownership enjoy the same legal status: social, co-operative, private, including foreign, as well as state ownership in the case of public enterprises. Another characteristic of the legislative changes is the principle of *national treatment* of foreigners i.e. the same legislation applies to both Yugoslav and foreign investors. A further component of the legislative changes is *deregulation*, where the autonomy of the firm is to market economy level. Then comes the principle of *universality*—the introduction of familiar and globally applied terms and categories which have proved to be efficient in the market economies. The laws accord *symmetrical treatment of labour and capital*. Enterprises are free to combine the two in order to maximize profit, and both participate in profit-sharing and decision-making.

3. Changes in economic trends

The next group of important conditions for definitely overcoming inflation is economic trends. When the current government assumed office in mid-March 1989, it could not take conclusive anti-inflationary measures owing to the low level of *foreign exchange reserves*, totalling approximately US$ 2.5 billion. Since then foreign exchange reserves increased considerably and amounted to over US$ 8.8 billion in July 1990.

The second material prerequisite for curbing inflation refers to *market supply*. Now that about 90 per cent of imports to Yugoslavia have been liberalized, an ample supply of home-produced and foreign commodities can be found on the Yugoslav market, which was not the case in the past.

4. The general anti-inflation model

In mid-December 1989 the government proposed to Parliament an integrated Programme of Economic Reform and Measures for its Implementation in 1990, consisting of (1) measures of economic policy; and (2) the so-called 'heterodox' shock measures.

4.1 Economic policy

Measures of economic policy rely on three principal levers: convertibility of the dinar, changes in fiscal policy and restrictive monetary policy.

(A) CONVERTIBILITY OF THE DINAR

Dinar convertibility has been introduced for all current external transactions. It was decided that the rate of exchange would be 7 dinars for 1 Deutschmark, and according to the current rates, this would mean about 12 dinars for 1 American dollar. The operation is based on pegging the dinar to the Deutschmark. Previously the dinar had been denominated by the ratio 1:10,000.

(B) FISCAL POLICY

Fiscal policy becomes much more prominent within the framework of economic policy. It had assumed many obligations so far carried out under monetary policy. Up to December 1989 the National Bank of Yugoslavia, by charging low interest rates on selective credits and beyond the official monetary limits, financed many priority activities: non-convertible exports, agriculture, export credits, etc. Therefore tasks of this type were transferred from the monetary to the fiscal sphere.

(C) MONETARY POLICY

The key task of monetary policy is *to keep the dinar convertible*. It is freed of many tasks which are now part of fiscal policy, thus making it possible for monetary policy to keep money supply in line with the tasks of economic policy, and, within that framework, the policy of convertibility. It is important that the monetary sphere does not issue too much money lest it impair the set Deutschmark/dinar ratio of 1:7.

4.2 'Heterodox shock'

The second group of measures is of the nature of a 'heterodox shock'. The aim is to blow out psychological inflation, i.e. inflationary expectations. This group of measures includes setting the upper limit of personal incomes for six months, and setting the upper limit of prices in infrastructure and public utilities for six months to about 25 per cent of producer prices. It was necessary to ensure that companies did not anticipate the cost-push effect and thus prepare to increase their output prices.

4.3 The results

The results of anti-inflation measures have been encouraging. The growth of retail prices fell from 65 per cent in December 1989 to 17 per cent in

January 1990, 8.2 per cent in February 1990, 2.6 per cent in March 1990, and to below 0 per cent in the April–June 1990 period. Foreign exchange reserves were increased by more than $5 billion.

5. Privatisation

The changes in economic system and anti-inflation results paved the way for property changes in Yugoslavia. In June 1990 the government launched a comprehensive privatization programme as the basis of a new development policy.

Despite the institutional provisions, the ownership restructuring of socially-owned enterprises had made little headway because the necessary prerequisites and mechanisms for this process had not been created. It was therefore necessary to amend the proposed concept of ownership restructuring as soon as possible, which implies the following: elimination of shortcomings of the Law on Social Capital (December 1989), a more detailed implementation of its provisions in the republican and provincial laws and intensification of the related promotional activities, which have been neglected so far.

The enhancement of the concept of ownershp restructuring and resolution of outstanding questions should be based on the following premises:

5.1 *Ownership restructuring* is not an end in itself, rather it is a means of increasing economic efficiency and a key link in the chain of the overall restructuring of the Yugoslav economy. It implies the transformation of social ownership into (1) public state ownership, i.e. nationalization; and (2) private ownership, i.e. privatisation. Since this is gradual process, it is necessary to create *parallel mechanisms*, which will secure the efficient utilization of the remaining social property in the transitional period.

5.2 *Nationalisation*, i.e. the transformation of social property into public property, is a simpler process and should be started without delay. There was a dilemma about whether social property should be transformed into public property by law or by the purchase of social capital by the state. The government chose the second solution.

5.3 With respect to *privatisation*, i.e. the transformation of social property into private property, the state should identify in the public sector all segments which are to be privatised, using methods and techniques known from the experience of other countries.

5.4 Another aim of privatisation should be the diversification of ownership, to embrace the broadest possible strata of the population. This will both create a broad coalition for a market-oriented economic development, and impact individual motivation of the employed and their identification with the enterprise.

5.5 Privatisation should not be confined either to distribution or to the sale of social capital. It has to be based on the *market concept*, relying on supply and demand and taking the cost of social capital into account.

5.6 Sectors to be transformed into public property

These are the sectors of major social concern, where instead of market competition, a natural monopoly prevails. The criteria for this identification should be simple and indisputable. It has been proposed that certain enterprises, classified as certain statistical sectors, should be entirely transformed into public property, which would then be followed by privatisation of areas where public ownership is not economically justified.

5.7 The rest of the economy to be privatised

This part of the economy should be grouped as follows:

(a) The *housing stock* should be privatised immediately, providing the possibility for payment of flats in instalments or by mortgages. This would be extremely important from the point of view of individual motivation.
(b) *Privatisation of enterprises which do not operate at a loss*, but whose efficiency would increase through privatisation.

The first step is to determine the *priority sectors* for privatisation. The starting criteria would have to include a considerable degree of competition, small enterprises and labour-intensive activities. These criteria are met by activities such as tourism, catering, trade, etc.

Second, it is necessary to *classify enterprises* within the priority sectors, e.g.:

—those ready for immediate privatisation;
—those which require minor revitalisation before being sold;
—those which require major revitalisation in order to be sold;
—those which are not suitable for sale.

In this connection, it should be borne in mind that it is extremely important for the first privatisation attempts to be 100 per cent successful.

(c) *Restructuring of enterprises operating with difficulties—large enterprises in particular*

An important form of rehabilitation of big enterprises is their segmentation into small and medium firms which would be privatised by the additional investment of private capital (dilution), or through the sale of parts or entire enterprises to private capital.

Conclusion

Yugoslavia is well into the reform, a fact recognised world-wide, and thus after some time, the confidence of the Yugoslav people has started to grow.

The results achieved so far will be used by the Yugoslav government to launch new initiatives in the political sphere. It is proposing changes in the constitution of SFRY, which are designed to abolish the leading role of the League of Communists and create conditions for the freedom of political association and direct multi-party secret elections.

Yugoslavia has now passed the turning-point. It is deep in an irreversible but smooth transformation or 'soft-landing' into market economy and multi-party democracy.

Živko Pregl
Vice-President of the Federal Executive Council
of the Socialist Federal Republic of Yugoslavia
Belgrade, July 1990

PREFACE

As I write this preface Yugoslavia is in turmoil. Federal, Serbian troops are skirmishing with Croatian and Slovenian militia. The Federation is on the brink of full-scale civil war and disintegration. This growing chaos has developed since Živko Pregl wrote his optimistic foreword to the book only last year.

Last year Živko Pregl could write confidently that the technical problems of the Yugoslav economy had been recognised and that a whole raft of reforms had been started in order to correct them. He predicted, optimistically as it turns out, that they would lead to peaceful change similar to that in some other East European states.

Why have these optimistic hopes been dashed by recent events? Among the complex causes of the current chaos in Yugoslavia two stand out as being particularly important. Both are discussed in the lessons that we draw in our concluding chapter. The first is nationalism. The second is the distribution of economic resources. It will be clear to anyone with a passing knowledge of Yugoslavia that it is the forceful reassertion of political and military nationalism among the republics that has embroiled them in bloody change. It is instructive to see how little the ideology of communism has been able to replace old conflicts based on history, religion and economics which made the Balkans, in the past, a bye-word for conflict in European history. There can be no doubt that nationalism is an important cause of Yugoslavia's current difficulties.

But, as we argue throughout the book, underlying national differences are even more important than differences in the distribution of economic resources. Another way of describing the current conflicts would be as economic wars between the richer northern republics and the poorer southern ones. Even under Tito, the resentment of the richer republics at federal redistribution of what they saw as their resources, to finance or subsidise southern industries, was barely concealed. We regard this as the most important single lesson to emerge from the book. Stated briefly, it is that distributional issues are at the heart of the problems of political economy and they have not been solved satisfactorily in communist regimes.

Having failed to reach satisfactory compromises on nationalist and economic issues the future for Yugoslavia is becoming daily more uncertain. Nobody can predict with certainty what the outcomes will be.

All one can say at this time is that some mutually exclusive alternatives are emerging. The first pair of these is the continuation of the Federation in some modified form or its break-up into separate groups of republics. The uncertainties here revolve around the ultimate lack of the necessary economic resources by Serbia to impose its military will on Croatia and Slovenia. On the other hand, Bosnia-Herzegovenia and Montenegro appear to be too poor to become viable states in their own right.

A second pair of mutually exclusive alternatives are the continuation in some form of the territorial integrity of Yugoslavia, or the disposal of some of its parts either to individual countries such as Italy, Greece and Albania, or to supra-national entities such as the European Community. The second alternative would create problematic precedents. It could reactivate all sorts of territorial claims in other parts of Europe. It could also activate cessationist claims from parts of other West European nations.

Both these pairs of mutually exclusive alternatives create problems for the European Community and any coordinated response to them. Clearly it is not in the Community's interests to have destabilised and violent nations on its borders. The history of (at the time) apparently obscure events, such as the assassination of Archduke Ferdinand at Sarajevo, will not be lost on today's Community.

In the same vein, the Community cannot contribute to that destabilisation nor create potential difficulties for its own members by interfering in the internal affairs of extra-Community nations. Such interference would include the recognition of parts of existing states as separate nations.

Recognition of these problems could lead to compromise politics of sticks and carrots. The carrots could be major planned aid to develop the Yugoslavian economy together with policies for progressive territorial distributions. The stick could be that before such assistance is forthcoming, the warring republics must reach political compromises that respect at least the overall territorial integrity of Yugoslavia even as a loose confederation rather than the current federation.

If such compromises could be reached, then the policies Živko Pregl was so optimistic would succeed, might still be given an opportunity to work in the decade.

James Simmie
Paris
August 1991

ACKNOWLEDGEMENTS

The comparative study of political economies of countries other than one's own is fraught with possibilities for misunderstanding. The combination of different historical traditions and languages makes it very difficult for outsiders to grasp the subtle realities of systems in which they do not live themselves. Eastern European political economies present the additional problem, until recently, of having experimented with systems that are particularly different from those with which most Western scholars are personally familiar. Thus, even in translation key concepts such as democracy, self-management, participation and social ownership immediately take on different meanings in different cultural experiences.

One of the best ways to overcome such problems is to ask scholars who have lived and worked in a given political economy to write about it and to provide explanations for those whose personal experiences have been gained elsewhere. In putting together this book we have been particularly fortunate in persuading some of Yugoslavia's leading intellectuals to write freely about key aspects of the country's government, economy and collective consumption.

The putting together of such a distinguished team has been the work of Jože Dekleva and colleagues at the Urban Planning Institute of Slovenia. Without the unstinting assistance of all concerned with this project in Yugoslavia this book could not have been written with such authority.

The Hayter Foundation and the British Council also provided invaluable funds to bring the different scholars together to work on the project. Without their assistance the work would have taken much longer and would probably have been overtaken by the pace of change in Yugoslavia.

Despite all their best endeavours the responsibility for any remaining faults and omissions remains with the editors. Nevertheless, we have gained a great deal of enjoyment and knowledge from working on the project. We hope that readers, both experts and interested observers alike, will also feel the same way about it.

James Simmie and Jože Dekleva
London, November 1990

PART I
INTRODUCTION

1 SELF-MANAGEMENT IN YUGOSLAVIA

James Simmie

Yugoslavia is a fascinating example of both a unique Communist party-dominated political economy, and a relatively accessible manifestation of the more general problems and deficiencies of such regimes. On the one hand its break with the Cominform in 1948 provided it with the unique opportunity to develop its own national communist political economy; on the other hand its problems of economic growth, distributional social justice and the eventual emergence of dissenting new social movements are fairly typical of those besetting other East European states.

This most important unique feature of the Yugoslav political economy is the concept and practice of self-management. At first sight it appears to be the antithesis of other East European systems. The constitutional changes of 1974, together with the Associated Labour Act of 1976, seemed to establish a decentralised and plural system of industrial, political, territorial and interest-delegated decision-making.

At work, firms (enterprises) were transformed into Basic Organisations of Associated Labour. These formed the basic economic decision-making cells. They were linked through their own local enterprise council to special delegations in the Assemblies of Associated Labour at both the commune and republican levels of government.

At home, the old small 'communes' were grouped into fewer larger ones to form the basic territorial political unit. Local self-management organisations provided delegates to the assemblies of associated labour and local communities, which, together with the assembly of socio-political organisations, made up the triumvirate of assemblies established at commune and republican levels.

Public services and infrastructure were provided by self-management interest communities. These were 'voluntary' combinations of self-managed producer enterprises and local communities. Delegates from the latter pursued local collective consumption interests.

An apparently plural polity was initiated by the formal recognition of five approved socio-political organisations. These are the League of Communists of Yugoslavia (SKJ) (this is the Communist party by another name); the Socialist Alliance of Working People of Yugoslavia; the Trade Unions Federation of Yugoslavia; the Veterans' Federation; and the League of Socialist Youth (SSOJ).

The book is devoted to an analysis of the self-management elements of the Yugoslav political economy. While it is easy to assume that genuine political pluralism cannot flourish in a one-party state, part of the legitimating ideology of communist regimes is their unique concern for workers and social equality. It therefore seems at least theoretically possible that a system vaunted as decentralised, bottom up and localised could produce more and progressively distributed benefits for local workers and residents within the confines of a communist one-party state. The Yugoslav contributors to this book argue that this has not been the case in practice.

Their analyses are divided into five main parts, including this introduction. Part II is devoted to the role of government and politics. All communist regimes are essentially the creation of military and political force. In the case of Yugoslavia, a liberation war against Nazi Germany was transformed into a social revolution. Once the initial military revolutions have been completed, the political role of the state is dominant. For this reason we start with these topics rather than with the economy where self-management was first introduced.

In Part II Janez Šmidovnik analyses the disfunctions of self-management in the economy, local communities and public administration. Zagorka Golubović critically evaluates whether self-management could ever have been genuine self-government under the conditions in which it was established in Yugoslavia. Tomaž Mastnak looks at the comparatively recent emergence of new social movements and political parties in Slovenia.

Janez Šmidovnik argues that the self-management of enterprises has suffered from four main problems. First, there was the problem of ownership. The second problem followed from the first. Where the state, directors and workers in enterprises did not accept ownership responsibilities, there was a tendency for them all to use the enterprise for their own different ends. The third problem was that under this system it was very difficult to make authoritative decisions in the light of any independent economic or managerial assessment of what they should be for any particular enterprise *per se*. The fourth problem identified by Janez Šmidovnik is the attempt to solve economic problems mainly within the political and organisational confines of the commune.

Local areas in Yugoslavia are divided into some 533 communes with an average population of about 42,000 inhabitants. They have become so overloaded with state functions that something like the old parishes, which they had replaced, had to be reinvented in order to deal with purely local government matters. Janez Šmidovnik concludes that local government just does not work in Yugoslavia.

The third subject to which he turns his attention is that of public administration. In the case of Yugoslavia this means the provision of collectively consumed services and goods such as social services and infrastructure. The institutional vehicles for achieving these ends were self-management interest communities. They have proved more or less incapable of providing adequate social services and infrastructure on their own and were consequently abolished.

Zagorka Golubović argues that genuine self-government is incompatible with one-party Marxist states. Real self-government requires a developed civil society separate and independent from the state. Tomaž Mastnak argues that the all-pervasive state, dominated by the Communist party, can only be reformed by separating the state and government from the party and introducing a pluralist party system.

In Slovenia and Croatia such a challenge has arisen on the bases of new social movements. These have included punks, pacifists, environmentalists, feminists, gays and spiritualists. Elements of the new social movements were transformed from independent social into independent political activities as a direct result of state and party attempts to repress freedom of expression. Free elections took place in 1990 in both Croatia and Slovenia for the first time since the Second World War.

Thus, government and politics are changing in Yugoslavia as elsewhere in Eastern Europe. The driving-force of this change is partly the political success of new political parties, and partly the result of the twin pressures of relative economic failure and continuing social inequalities. We address both these issues in Parts III and IV.

In Part III Jože Mencinger and Bogomir Kovač analyse the problems of economic growth and change. They show how economic problems have driven political reforms and how the limits of Marxist adaptations to inadequate economic performance have been reached. They also identify some of the technical difficulties involved in changing a socialist economy back into a market economy.

Jože Mencinger argues that poor economic performance, as much as anything else, led to the reform programme launched in 1988. Its objectives were no less than to create new integral product, labour and capital markets. He points out that these are incompatible with social property and self-management. The stage has been set for a full-scale return to capitalism.

Bogomir Kovač examines one of the major problems involved in changing from a collective to a market economy. This is the complex technical problem of turning a Basic Organisation of Associated Labour into a capitalist, market organisation. Proposals for reform have included tighter financial controls and entrepreneurial development. Both pose major technical difficulties.

All these emerging changes lead Bogomir Kovač to argue that social ownership is a socialist relic. He and Jože Mencinger both show collective, socialist solutions to running the Yugoslav economy and its individual enterprises/associations have foundered upon poor economic performance.

In Part IV we turn to the issue of social justice and social policy. Barbara Verlič-Dekleva discusses why Yugoslav social policy has been so limited in its effects on equality; Pavel Gantar and Srna Mandič illustrate the lack of social equality in housing allocations; and Ognjen Čaldarović looks at urban social inequality. Taken together the three analyses show how inequality has persisted and even been re-created under self-managed Yugoslavian communism.

Barbara Verlič-Dekleva addresses the phenomenon of the overlap between economic and social policy. She points out that although human and social equality were major objectives of the post-war transformation of Yugoslavia, they have not been achieved in practice. Yugoslav social policy has not been a means of reducing social inequalities. After nearly half a century of the communist experiment major inequalities persist between regions, workers, those without work and those confined to the 'grey' economy.

Pavel Gantar and Srna Mandič examine the effects of communist housing policies and their contribution to social equality. Shortages in housing supply have persisted. The formal construction sector is unable to supply enough housing. Workers have therefore been left to build their own accommodation. A large, informal self-build sector has developed in most major cities. Major housing inequalities have therefore emerged between those in more desirable social housing and those in self-build accommodation.

In urban areas, Ognjen Čaldarović shows that inequalities in location are added to those of housing quality to produce further social inequality in cities. He reports research findings which show that different social status groups were in possession of different housing rights, and that in Zagreb higher social status groups were found concentrated disproportionately in central areas, while workers were more often concentrated on the periphery.

We conclude from these analyses that for most practical purposes, the abolition of social classes defined according to Marx has not removed social inequalities in communist societies such as Yugoslavia. As far as most people's everyday lives are concerned, social status and party distinctions continue to be the bases of significant social and material inequalities.

Finally, in Part V the editors, James Simmie and Jože Dekleva extract the lessons that emerge from the analyses both for Yugoslavia and other

East European political economies now in the complex process of transforming themselves into market economies. We emphasise four main considerations.

The first is that in one-party states such as those dominated by communist parties, much of what takes place must be legitimately laid at the door
of 'the party'. However, events have more complex causes and effects than
only those that can be attributed to 'the party'.

Second, and following from this point, social and ideological constraints
within particular nations need to be considered in the explanation of the
forms and outcomes of government actions.

Third, most communist experiments, and here Yugoslavia is no excep-
tion, are bounded by existing economic and political possibilities. Not
even single-party states are entirely free to pursue their 'utopian' experiments without any constraints.

Finally, we also argue that, to paraphrase John Donne, no nation is an
island. Thus both Yugoslavia and other nations-states in Eastern Europe
have had to adjust not only to conditions at home but also to those abroad.

Despite these caveats, the general verdict of our Yugoslav writers on
self-management echoes that of a recent English analysis of the political
crisis in Yugoslavia. That was summarised in the following terms:

The Party [has used] the other four socio-political organisations as a platform for
expressing its own views, as a source of statements and resolutions supporting
party policy, and as instruments for implementing that policy. Except on rare
occasions, and then only briefly, these organisations never show the slightest sign
of independent thought or action. They contribute practically nothing to the
much-vaunted idea of Yugoslavia as a superior kind of democratic society, in
which there is a 'pluralism of self-management interests'. (Lydall, 1989, p. 21)

One final consideration which should be borne in mind while following
the analyses in this book is how far the more or less universal collapse of
communist regimes in Eastern Europe strikes at the very heart of Marxist
theory. Most of them, including Yugoslavia, were established on the basis
of this theory and its Leninist, Soviet interpretations. No other social scien-
tist has had his ideas used in such a long and extensive social experiment. At
the end of the day the experiment appears to have failed. This must indicate
that there are serious flaws in the original ideas themselves as well as their
execution in practice.

The analyses presented here cast serious doubt on the validity of three
Marxist concepts in particular. These are the significance he attributes to the
role of private property, the relevance of his conception of a 'classless'
society, and the direction of history.

The role of private property in capitalist societies is seen by Marx as
one which forms the basis of a set of exploitative social relationships

between owners and non-owners. This overrides other considerations. The Yugoslav experience has shown that the abolition of private productive economic property only serves to introduce different forms of exploitation and extremely inefficient use of such resources. Even in the self-management system of economic decision-making, major decisions and resulting benefits remained in the hands of the political and managerial élites. When workers tried to acquire more of the comparatively rare surpluses generated in their 'own' enterprises, they were eventually prevented from receiving them on the basis of the familiar and 'correct' argument that they were required for essential investments to generate future economic growth. One of the workers' main responses to this dilemma has been to expand greatly the informal or 'black' economy. Estimates in this volume put this at somewhere between 30 and 40 per cent of gross domestic product.

The inefficient use of 'socially owned' resources is legendary. The lack of private owners of some kind seems to remove much concern for the responsible use of those resources. The benefits of multiple, decentralised and efficient decision-making under conditions of private ownership appear to outweigh those of 'social ownership'. In the case of Yugoslavia these are indicated by the fact that the national economy has grown by 30 per cent less than comparable Southern European market economies since the Second World War.

Marx's concept of a classless society rested on the connections between the ownership of property and his particular definition of social class. The abolition of private property axiomatically produced a classless society in this concept. This however has not proved to be a particularly significant change in Yugoslavia, or indeed, elsewhere. The definitional abolition of social classes has by no means removed equally important forms of social stratification in the everyday lives of those living in communist regimes.

Social status groups and the party have continued to form the basis of a system of social stratification. Again from the point of view of many workers' everyday lives, distributional inequalities generated in a social class system are experienced in much the same ways in communist status and party systems. Relatively low incomes and poor housing conditions contribute to very similar life experiences regardless of the theoretical system in which they have been generated.

Finally, Marx's belief that an historical progression from classical through feudal and capitalist societies to a socialist nirvana was inevitable or even taking place, appears to be completely misplaced. Recent experiences throughout Eastern Europe indicate that the Marxist socialist experiment has been a failure and is drawing to a close. If it is indeed replaced by contemporary forms of capitalism, this calls into question Marx's entire theory of history and its material causes.

These theoretical issues raise not just the technical questions of how to transform communist collective political economies into market pluralist democracies. They also raise the problem of how to break out of nearly a century and a half of Marxist-inspired or influenced thought. Many bodies of social thought, including economics, politics, sociology and philosophy, comprise a large proportion of discourse that depends upon the concepts and language of Marx and his followers. In communist regimes these have been the only permitted concepts and language. They have led to deformed debate and retarded the advancement of knowledge in religious proportions.

One task that emerges from the current changes is how to confine Marxist thought to the history of ideas. At the same time much attention needs to be focused on the problem of how to develop new theories and modes of thought to understand and explain the new societies emerging in Eastern Europe. At the moment their practices are well in advance of theories to understand and interpret them.

In this book we describe and analyse the practices of self-management in Yugoslavia. It has been a unique European contribution to communist regimes in the Third World. It deserves the attention given to it here as one of the few options devised to centralised Stalinist systems. That even self-management has failed is a clear indication that the entire communist project is nearing its end.

Reference

Lydall, H. (1989) *Yugoslavia in Crisis*, Oxford, Clarendon Press.

PART II
GOVERNMENT AND POLITICS

INTRODUCTION

James Simmie

In Part II we examine a key problem for Marxist theory and communist regimes alike. The problem is how could the state wither away as long as a dominant role is required by the communist party to establish its objectives and to set up and organise government means to achieve those objectives?

In Yugoslavia, the early attempts to develop elements of a self-managed market economy in the helpful context of world economic growth soon challenged the monopolistic position of the Communist party. Important economic decisions could be taken by firms and workers without reference to the party and the state. While this could be seen as a 'withering away' of state functions, it was not allowed by the party to continue.

The 1974 constitutional reforms and the 1976 Associated Labour Act on the one hand established the system of self-management as it existed until the end of the 1980s, and on the other hand it reinstated the state and the Communist party at the heart of all significant decisions. Janez Šmidovnik analyses the problems of self-management during this period in its three main institutional settings: enterprises, communes and public services.

Janez Šmidovnik argues that the self-management of enterprises has suffered from four main problems. First, there was the question of ownership. The Marxist assumption that revolutionary changes in economic property ownership would axiomatically benefit economic performance and labour has proved to be naïvely optimistic. In practice the private ownership of economic property was transformed into a system in which neither institutions nor individuals took up all the rights and responsibilities of ownership. This meant that in effect, Yugoslav enterprises have had no real owners of any kind.

The second problem followed from the first. Where the state, directors and workers in enterprises did not accept ownership responsibilities there was an inclination for some of them to use the enterprise for their own ends. The state as represented by the Communist party intervened continually in attempts to maintain some progress towards its utopian objectives. Directors represented a political stronghold in the enterprise, and while following party instructions also tended to aim mainly for a 'quiet life'. Workers proved to have little interest or ability to manage firms. Their main aim was to obtain the highest possible wages compatible with the least responsibility for decision-making.

The third problem was that under this system it was very difficult to make authoritative decisions in the light of any independent economic or managerial assessment of requirements for any particular enterprise *per se*. The result is that many enterprises do not break even in strict accounting terms. Risk and debt have been absorbed by the banks, again under political direction by the party through the state.

The fourth problem identified by Janez Šmidovnik is the attempt to solve economic and social problems, mainly within the political and organisational confines of the commune. This is both the basic political and economic cell in the Yugoslav political economy. It has ensured both the geographic fragmentation of enterprises and constant state intervention in them.

The commune in Yugoslavia has been developed from the conceptual example of the Paris Commune of 1871 as described by Marx. It is a fairly small territorial unit originally based on old parish boundaries. Most functions of the state are fragmented and devolved to self-management institutions in individual communes. Janez Šmidovnik points out that there are some 533 communes in all, with an average population of about 42,000 inhabitants. They became so overloaded with state functions that something like the old 'parishes', which they had replaced, had to be reinvented in order to deal with purely local government matters. These were called local communities.

Both within and between these government units decisions are supposed to be made on the basis of consensus expressed in compacts. The interconnection of political and economic decision-making means that many of these compacts are confused in their objectives and uncoordinated in their execution. Local communities do not have the resources or staff to overcome these problems at the very local level. As a result, Janez Šmidovnik concludes that local government just does not work according to theoretical expectations in Yugoslavia.

The third and final subject to which he turns his attention is that of public administration. In the case of Yugoslavia this means the provision of collectively consumed services and goods such as social services and infrastructure. Influenced by Marxist doctrine on the withering away of the state, services and goods such as these were supposed to be provided by voluntary co-operation between those who could provide them and those who needed them. This excluded the necessity of state intervention.

The institutional vehicles for achieving these ends were self-management interest communities, which were introduced between 1970 and 1980. Their theoretical basis was that there would be a 'free exchange of labour' between suppliers and consumers, who would negotiate between themselves exactly what was needed. The money to pay for services and infrastructure would be raised from 'voluntary' contributions made by enterprises and also deducted from wages.

Among the problems confronting the self-management interest communities were, first, that in the poorer communes enterprises and workers were often unable to make adequate contributions for the provision of their own services. The republics found it virtually impossible to make progressive redistributions of funds to enable them to do so. Second, the self-management interest communities never managed to operate successfully without state intervention. If anything, they demonstrated the practical impossibility of the withering away of the state. As a result of these fundamental difficulties the organisations are themselves in decline and withering away.

Zagorka Golubović concludes that genuine self-management is incompatible with one-party Marxist states such as Yugoslavia. She contrasts the concept of self-government with that of self-management as practised in Yugoslavia. Real self-government requires a developed civil society separate and independent from the state. Communist regimes have prevented such developments because they are rightly seen as posing challenges to the unfettered domination of all aspects of life by the party.

In Yugoslavia the novel introduction of self-management in enterprises, local government and social services was imposed from above, over time, by ex-Stalinists, after the break with the Soviet Union. It was not the result of grass-roots social movements such as those which are forcing major changes in Yugoslavia in the 1990s. As such, self-management was a device to legitimise the continuing domination of the Communist party behind a façade of apparently decentralised and democratic decision-making. Nevertheless, as Zagorka Golubović says, the real power structure remained the same.

A key test of where power lies is the distributional outcomes of economic and political decisions. We show, in Part IV, that inequalities in social security and services have been maintained under self-management. Zagorka Golubović also notes a shift in the balance of power from enterprises and towards the state in terms of the distribution of economic resources. The distributional question emerges as one of the most significant in this critique of self-management. On a more general level it also strikes at the heart of communist claims about social justice and equality.

A final paradox of self-management is that in its name, independent workers' social movements and trade unions have been stifled in Yugoslavia. Self-management was not allowed to develop into self-government in the factories and offices. Various reasons and difficulties have been advanced to explain this apparent paradox. Zagorka Golubović concludes, however, that self-management as self-government could never have worked in Yugoslavia as long as the Communist party clung to power.

Tomaž Mastnak argues that the all-pervasive state, dominated by the Communist party, can be reformed by separating the state and government from the party and introducing a pluralist party system. In Slovenia and Croatia such a challenge has arisen on the basis of new social movements. The early stages of this challenge did not confront powerful state institutions head on. Indeed, the first example of a new social movement was the punk youth subculture, which was essentially irreverent and mocked communism. In retrospect it appears as more of a symbolic than a real challenge. By the 1980s it was followed by the manifestation of other movements which included pacifists, environmentalists, feminists, gays and spiritualists. As in the West, the role of the mass media in spreading the ideas of these movements, and thereby gathering support for them, was crucial. In Slovenia Radio Student and the official youth magazine 'The Youth' were particularly important.

Also as in the West, the active support of intellectuals and professional groups was significant in the development of the new social movements. They were able to articulate the problem of re-creating a civil society entirely separate from the state. They were also able to make use of legal arguments to constrain the more extreme state actions within a legal framework and a semblance of rational discourse.

Despite attempts at repression even from local residents and workers, the youth subculture emerged in party discourse in 1985. Attempts were made to absorb it into Marxist theory and find a role for it within the existing institutions. However, Tomaž Mastnak claims that by this time the youth were already lost to the party. Elements of the new social movements were transformed from independent social into independent political activities as a direct result of state and party attempts to repress freedom of expression. This was attempted in Slovenia in 1988 when some editors, a writer and an army NCO were put on trial in Ljubljana charged with revealing a military document.

The trial sparked off the formation of a Committee for the Defence of Human Rights. This rapidly gained support. There was even support from the liberal faction of the party. It also provided a focus for independent political activity. The experience gained in this activity provided inspiration and opportunities for the formation of independent political parties, which soon followed.

In 1990 free elections took place in both Croatia and Slovenia for the first time since the Second World War. It is doubtful if this would have been the case without the prior existence of the new social movements. There is no evidence that the Communist party would have relinquished power or the state withered away without the intervention of such human agents.

2 DISFUNCTIONS OF THE SYSTEM OF SELF-MANAGEMENT IN THE ECONOMY, IN LOCAL TERRITORIAL COMMUNITIES AND IN PUBLIC ADMINISTRATION

Janez Šmidovnik

Introduction

Judging from the current situation in Yugoslavia, it may be concluded that the self-management system, or even the idea of self-management itself was, right from the beginning, a misconception, the very reason for the catastrophic socialist system in Yugoslavia, and an imminent threat to the existence of the state itself. Nevertheless, there are established arguments to the contrary.

With the introduction of self-management in the economy, Yugoslavia enjoyed, from 1950 onwards, a period of economic and political prosperity, and, right through to the 1970s was far ahead, in every respect, of all the other socialist states that retained the Soviet state-administrative system of economic management and management of all other activities. This was the time of relative prosperity, a high degree of economic development and increasing individual freedom of the people. During this period, Yugoslavia was a kind of experimental polygon which attracted attention in scientific and political circles around the world, for it appeared that it had established a promising model of socialism, which could eventually be acceptable in international relations, or possibly even as an example for specific societies—at least in the underdeveloped countries.

Where, then, lay the basis of these initial successes? Self-management could not have functioned without prior denationalisation, without separation of economic subjects (enterprises) from the state. The legal divorce from the state and its budget, and the economic independence of enterprises, in itself allowed for the realisation of a market economy, though still under the strong control of the state. Notwithstanding all the initial shortcomings of the system, this very circumstance offered the Yugoslav economy such drift that in a few years, the whole image of the country was completely different from the Soviet type of socialist states.

This development was, however, sharply interrupted in the 1970s by the leadership of the Communist party, which managed the whole project of Yugoslav socialism. The leadership felt that the social development (particularly in the economic field) which was taking place, was beginning to threaten their monopolistic position. The position of the party, which had retained all the essential characteristics of the monopolistic 'Lenin party', was really under threat. As a result of the new economic system, the prospering economy was gaining social and political power and damaging the party, which was becoming dispensable as the system was squeezing it out to the edges of society.

Political measures, therefore, had to be taken, which would turn the trend of development back to the administrative management of the economy and the political regulation of public administration, thus reinstalling both spheres under the control of the party.

The party took advantage of some negative effects that had resulted from the previous system based on the market and self-management. One such effect was rising social differentiation, while the main one was the surfacing of some nationalistic tendencies in a multinational communal state, in particular the so-called Croatian 'MASPOK' in the 1970s.

Using the excuse of the 'threatened self-management system', the party put in action a series of measures with which it effectively limited self-management and also restricted the market autonomy of economic organisations. These measures were constitutionally sanctioned by the 1974 constitution, and later executed in detail, especially by the Associated Labour Act of 1976.

State administration in the economic field was thus reinstated, particularly in the form of the 'social negotiation' between business subjects, intended to replace previous 'market disorder'. This saw the introduction of the regime of the 'negotiated economy', which allowed the party ample opportunity for intervention in the economic and all other social spheres. With this began the collapse of the Yugoslav economy and society.

The self-management system in the economy

In the economy the self-management system was inadequate right from the start and ought to have undergone early major improvement. The fundamental problem was property ownership. The Yugoslav Communist party (like all the other communist parties, with the Soviet party in the lead), had adopted as its basic doctrine the notion of the social utopias of the nineteenth century, which was expressed in the motto 'property ownership is theft'. Private ownership of the means of production is, according to this notion, the basis for the capitalistic exploitation of 'man against man', and the very essence of the exploitative nature of the capitalist social order.

Nationalisation of the means of production was therefore one of the first measures taken by the new socialist leaderships in all the countries that adopted the Soviet model of socialism. The nationalisation was radical. It included all the economic and non-economic spheres—engulfing industrial giants as well as the smallest country inn. This measure, however, soon led to several disfunctions, the first being an immense administrative bureaucratisation, and productive inefficiency of the whole system. Despite these shortcomings, all the systems insisted on maintaining state ownership, with only limited laxity in favour of a few private activities in agriculture and certain areas of small industry.

In respect of nationalisation Yugoslavia went a step further. It expropriated all state property formerly managed by enterprises and other organisations, into *social property*. Essentially, social property was supposed to be administered by the working collectives of the self-managing enterprises, and not by the state. However, the nature and legal status of social property were, on the other hand, never clearly defined. Throughout the period after the declaration of social property, the question continually arose, in legal and economic theory, as well as in practice of what 'social property' really was; how it differed from state property on the one hand, and from private property on the other. Whose property was it?

The state arbitrated on the whole matter, overseeing all economic activities involving public property, particularly the financial side of the economy (above all the distribution of income), through its regulations. The state also intervened directly in the management of enterprises, especially in the appointment of directors, through whom it was then possible to influence operational decisions. Such influence would be executed via the 'commune' which, in the new organisation, was no longer just a local territorial community, but rather a commune (as envisaged by Marx) which was, at the same time, meant to be the basic economic cell of society. Thus, the state assured itself of the necessary income from enterprises on the one hand, and political influence on the other, which would ensure the development of 'real' socialism. The state discontinued the management of public property, failed to execute ownership rights in this respect, and did not behave as a responsible owner. In this way, the state ceased to be the owner of enterprises. On the other hand, neither did the working collectives become the owners of enterprises and, therefore they too did not behave as responsible owners.

The system operated in such a way that success in enterprises was not primarily the result of effort and good management of the working collectives but, above all, of state measures, particularly the distributive mechanism, i.e. the system of income distribution between the state and the enterprises. Success was also a result of the skilfulness of the director and other senior officers who managed to find their way through these state 'instruments'.

In short, the self-management enterprise has no owner, while social property is, up to now, mostly still distinguished as 'no-property', in other words, something that has no owner. It belongs neither to the state or to an individual, nor is it owned by working collectives. Social property has no title ownership. While the state executes particular ownership rights, and the working collective other rights, there is no title-holder who would carry the responsibility for the good management of the property.

Because of the Yugoslav system of self-management, property could be neither state nor privately owned, while the third form, i.e. social property, never turned out to be an appropriate basis for efficient management. The early period after the introduction of self-management nevertheless saw a prosperous management of social property, mainly under the authority of directors. Workers' self-management was mostly exercised in the form of formal approvals of the directors' proposals.

The question of property ownership, however, was raised right from the beginning, and not as an abstract question but rather as:

1. a matter of responsibility for the success of the enterprise;
2. a matter of the absence of enterprise risk in the management of social property; and
3. a matter of the inflation generated by this ownerless model of enterprise.

In order to ensure a sense of responsibility in the organisation, two subjects are required. First, there needs to be a *sanctioning subject*, who may demand responsibility and is also capable of achieving it; and second, a *responsibility subject*, who must be able to carry responsibility—in this case, the responsibility to manage social property.

The Yugoslav system of self-management lacks both. The sanctioning subject should operate to realise the interests of the owners. However, we have seen that under the Yugoslav system there are neither state nor working collective owners. Nor is there any responsibility subject, since the working collective is not and cannot be qualified in this capacity. The director, too, cannot be the responsibility subject, since his position in the organisation is that of an executive organ of the working collective, or rather, its workers' council. He is not, generally, responsible for the management of social property.

As for the working collectives, it is characteristic of them that, notwith-standing their formally declared self-managing role, they behave like organs of wage workers and not like managers. As individuals and as management collectives, the workers always demand the highest salaries, irrespective of company success. It has been undisputedly established in daily self-management practice, as well as in empirical studies, that Yugoslav workers carry no responsibility for the management of social property, and are mainly interested only in their salaries. Responsibility for the enterprise far transcends their capabilities, intellectual and material, as well as their aspirations. This means that in a system of social property, like that of Yugoslavia, it is impossible to realise a structure of responsi-bility. Self-management enterprise simply just does not have any owner. It therefore follows that in such a system there is no need to worry about good management, development, innovation, and constant growth in busi-ness. Statistical data, for instance, reveals that Yugoslavia is at the bottom of the European chart of inventions, patents, innovations, and so on.

In view of these revelations, there arises the question of enterprise risk. Who carries enterprise risk in the self-management system? Enterprise risk is an unavoidable component of all business decisions in market economies: there is no business without enterprise risk. Enterprise risk acts as an instrument that protects business, or rather, managers from taking rushed and insufficiently considered decisions. Every false move backfires on to the decision-maker.

In the ownerless Yugoslav system, however, risk does not strike the manager or decision-maker. The working collective—or its workers' council— cannot carry the risk, although it takes decisions (at least formally) on all important management issues such as investments. Yugoslav practice has seen countless faulty investments that have, at times, shaken the whole country, without directly affecting those who made the decisions, or took part in the decision-making. The director does not carry any risk since the important decisions are approved by the workers' council, or with his con-sent; neither do the government and party officials, who frequently influence decision-making in enterprises, carry any responsibility or risk for those decisions, since it is not their job anyway.

As such, this system of management offers no protection from the dangers associated with the management of social property. Society must there-fore bear the consequences of the lack of these safeguards, since all the damage done by individual subjects of management is absorbed by the whole of society.

The next unfavourable consequence of such a system may be exemplified by the inflationary effect of the economic system. Self-man-agement enterprise has a built-in lust for inflation. The workers, and the working collectives, are always demanding the highest pay, irrespective of enterprise success. The director is forced to submit to their demands.

Higher pay causes higher expenditure, and likewise, higher prices, which the monopolistically closed economy legitimises and approves. There is nobody, in this mechanism, who could stop price-rises through enterprise competition on the market; everyone stamps on the accelerator, while there is no brake pedal. The result is innate inflation and economic instability, which are characteristic of such a mechanism.

As these characteristics of the self-management of social property became more evident, so also was there an increase in the excessive power of political demogogy, as opposed to professional principles of management. This was the case after the 1974 Constitution, especially during recent years. The fact that property ownership is the most difficult problem in the Yugoslav system of self-management has been clearly demonstrated recently in connection with the so-called 'Marković Economic Reform', whereby the former economic system is supposed to have been transformed into a market economy. This move ought to separate those who are capable of operating in a competitive market from those who are not. It has been discovered that it is impossible to develop a consistent market system on the basis of social property, or in other words, that a social property economy cannot be competitive in the market. This is not difficult to understand in view of the disfunctions of the social property regime, already discussed.

Marković had, *ipso facto*, to start by allowing for the re-establishment of private property in the economy and by ensuring the transformation of social property either into private or state property in various forms. This was effected by the 'Law on Enterprises' of 1989. Although this law did not abolish social property as a special ownership category, it did, however, put an end to its monopolistic status. Most economists are of the opinion that social property will wipe itself out. Because of its uncompetitive nature, it will cease to exist, and the appropriate assets will shift into the hands of private or state owners.

The second set of disfunctions is in the technical organisation itself of the realisation of the concept of self-management. The centre of all self-management decision-making was supposed to be directly with the working collective. According to the already mentioned Law on Associated Labour, which, at the time of its inception (1976), was identified even in political circles as a 'mini workers' constitution', decisions on the most important issues of management are made by the workers of enterprises either directly through a referendum, or any other direct means of declaration. On other issues of management, decisions are made in workers' councils, which are elected from within and represent all levels of the working collective. In this way, workers take direct decisions by referendum on every issue concerning the merging or linkage with other organisations; on all administrative changes within the organisation; on the basis for annual and long-term production programmes of the organisation; on the criteria for the distribution of funds for salaries and for the general expenditure of the working collective; and on all the other issues defined by the statute of the management of the enterprise, which is itself, likewise approved by the workers by referendum. Apart from this, the working collective must be considered and must always give its opinion on every proposed negotiation for a loan agreement for investment.

As the organ of the working collective, the workers' council on the other hand, by law, approves all the regulations by which working and other relations are conducted in the enterprise. It also determines the business policy of the enterprise, and sets measures for its implementation; approves the production plan; decides on the taking of credit; approves periodical settlements and final accounts; appoints and dismisses the director; and it is also its duty to give him working guidelines and supervise his work.

In this way, the director's work ought to be guided by and be dependent on the working collective, for he is only its executive organ. The director, whose role may also be played by the board of directors, runs the daily operations of the enterprise; organises the working process; proposes the business policy of the enterprise; and executes the decisions taken by the working collective and workers' council. The director sits in on the meetings of the workers' council, though with no voting rights. He is directly answerable to the workers' council. The workers' council may discharge him at any time, should it find his work inadequate. The move to discharge him may be initiated by the workers themselves, the relevant 'commune', the syndicate, or the self-management public prosecutor.

The working collective of the self-management enterprise, therefore, does not only play the role of owner of the enterprise, but also that of the direct management of the enterprise. This means that it executes functions which, in other parts of the world, are entrusted only to a professional manager. The director, as its executive organ, only assists in the execution of current daily operations, since the working collective cannot physically carry them out. In this way, the idea of self-management in the form of direct workers' decision-making was expected to have become firmly established.

Understandably, a self-management mechanism formulated in this way could not function successfully. It is obvious that working collectives just could not successfully, and responsibly, decide on such a wide spectrum of management issues, because

1. they are not the owners of the enterprise and do not feel any responsibility for their fate;
2. they are not, and cannot be, competent for management, which is a highly demanding professional activity;
3. most workers do not have any wish to manage enterprises as that far exceeds the level of their aspirations.

On the other hand, nor can the director effectively and successfully run a self-managed enterprise. His functioning is, in all important aspects, formally tied to the working collective and the workers' council, as well as, virtually, to the commune and party to which, more often than not, he owes his appointment to the job. The director, therefore, cannot run the enterprise according to the professional standards of modern management, but rather, on the amateur criteria of the working collective, together with strong political influence from the commune and the party. Within the provided framework, the director too is not, and cannot be, responsible for company success; he lacks individual power, competence, and in most cases, knowledge too. His function is political rather than professional—it is, at any rate, a political stronghold in the enterprise. The director may always avoid responsibility for enterprise failure, since all major decisions are taken by the working collective and workers' council.

All this means that self-management enterprise is not aware of modern management as a professional activity that is becoming more and more professionalised. Yugoslav management is an amateur activity, which may be mostly classified as political activity and which may be conducted at the level of general decision-making by the working collective and workers' council. It follows, therefore, that every worker may take part in it, while at the level of daily management, executed by the director, is a predominantly political figure with the appropriate political qualifications—especially loyalty to the party. Although the director is formally appointed by the workers' council, only those with established political loyalty may be considered for the office.

Thus, in the Yugoslav self-management enterprise, we have political instead of professional management. Such management simply is not primarily aimed at efficiency and company success, profit and development; but it is rather content just with survival and social tranquillity in the enterprise.

As a result of the division of managerial obligations, the self-management mechanism cannot provide for the successful operation of an enterprise. Decision-making is an extremely complicated and very long process, which normally takes place with the painstaking efforts of the director to convince the working collective, or workers' council, about particular decisions which may be, in his opinion, absolutely necessary. These decisions, on the other hand, are in most cases in opposition to the workers' interests, and therefore inappropriate, in their opinion, for the satisfaction of their short-term direct benefits.

Under these circumstances, outside intervention from the state—the commune and party—is almost certain. The director who operates with state or party authority, stands a better chance of putting his ideas into practice than one without any such authority. This renders outside intervention part of the self-management system. All important decisions concerning enterprises had to be, until recently, accepted or even approved (informally), outside the enterprise. Without external intervention, the self-management system simply would not have functioned.

This presents us with an additional aspect, in view of which it may be stated that the self-management system operates without any sense of responsibility. None of the mentioned organs taking decisions in this system, is or can be responsible for the decisions taken. The working collective and workers' council cannot be responsible, despite the fact that they decide on very important issues, as these decisions far exceed their competence in every respect. The director cannot be responsible either, since his decisions are normally covered by the solutions and the consent of the workers' council. Nor can the 'commune' or party official carry the responsibility, though he might have eventually (informally) taken the decision, for it is not his constitutional right to decide.

As we saw, in the case of public property, the new law on enterprises introduced vital changes with respect to the self-management mechanism, if indeed it continues to operate at all. It may continue to operate, though, in state, public and mixed ownership enterprises. Under the new law, the authority of working collectives and workers' councils has been considerably limited in favour of more authority for the director. It has only recently been realised in Yugoslavia that there is a need for the professional management of the economy and other activities. Various institutions have therefore been founded for the education of managers, as is common practice in the Western world.

Self-management in local communities

In local communities, which classically fall under the sphere of territorial self-management, the system was supposed to be conducted in a certain way, in accordance with the specific Yugoslav system, i.e. the so-called 'communal system'. The communal system was introduced by the special law of 1955, by which the 'parish' in Yugoslavia ceased to be an institution of classical local self-management. It became a commune, which, according to the definition of the main party ideologist, Edvard Kardelj, meant 'an integrated social and economic community of all the inhabitants and organisations (including enterprises) in its territory'.

In the commune, all the fundamental economic, social, and political issues (e.g. issues of investment based on social property), are resolved through self-management. The commune is the basic cell of Yugoslav society, in which, in principle, all the needs of the community members and organisations, as producers and consumers, are satisfied. All the other forms of the state—regions, republics and the federation—are founded on the commune, which is built on the conceptual example of the Paris Commune of 1871, as described in Marx's analysis.

The commune is a model of a new way of organising society. This is a society of self-management without state compulsion. Communal organisation was expected to exert a strong influence on the structure of the whole state—from the parish to the peak of state administration (see J. Šmidovnik, Koncepcija Jugoslovanske občine, Ljubljana, Uradni list SRS, 1970, str. 126–36, 189–94).

Such nebulous ideology of the commune was, in the operational sense, later put into practice through the constitution and laws in such a way that the 'parish', as a commune, was declared the basic 'socio-political community' (SPC). The SPC was responsible for the management of all public matters in its territory, be it matters of local or general national importance. All together, in Yugoslav terminology, these units formed the state—regions, republics and the federation.

By constitution, the 'parish' also executed all national laws and all the other rules of state organs at the first level. This resulted in an avalanche of state duties on the communes, which, because of their limited territorial boundaries, they were unable to execute. There was a need for considerable territorial and organisational expansion. In fact, in the following years they grew almost to the level of the former counties, which had been abolished.

Today, there are 533 communes in Yugoslavia, which means that the average area of a commune is 479.93 square kilometres with an average population of 42,072, making it by far the largest commune in Europe. Its size may be compared with that of the territorial units of the second grade, which are normally national units (eg. the German Kreis or smaller English districts).

The commune also had to adapt its organisational structure to its new duties. It was granted by the constitution the same political organs as all the other socio-political communities, i.e. a parliament with three assemblies, an executive council, administrative organs, etc. The nature of the commune was most clearly exemplified in the new structure of management, based on the same departmental organisational principle of state management. Services of general national importance predominated in the commune (eg. matters of national defence, police, taxation, etc.), whereas there were no services for the operation of local matters (municipal activities, micro-economy, social activities, etc.).

It is undisputable today that the functioning of a commune is just an extension of the state apparatus, as its first level of operation. It has long ceased to be a local self-management community. In accordance with its new functional and territorial organisation, it has distanced itself from local communities and local matters, which it is no longer capable of running. It has had to abandon local matters to the 'local communities', which came into being as a kind of substitute for the former 'parishes', normally within the territorial boundaries of the previous small 'parishes'. The constitution itself recognises the local community and its organisation, but does not grant it the position of the former 'parishes'. Local communities are, in their legal status, a form of field amateur organisation, with an extremely loose structure. They have neither compulsory duties, nor constant revenues. Their functioning is mostly dependent on the initiative and amateur drive of some of the inhabitants, who may be, from time to time, very active, or may also be entirely passive. In short, as an institution, the local community cannot perform those public duties on which the development of settlements in a modern country depends, with certainty and to the appropriate standard.

It is quite clear today that the communal system has not succeeded, and that its concept could not be realised since it was, right from the beginning, in contrast to the Yugoslav system itself, and especially contrary to the effort to consolidate self-management in the economy.

Self-management of the economy demanded the divorce of the enterprise from the state, while communal organisation allows the (voluntary) intervention of the commune into economic matters. Particularly unsuccessful was the attempt to transform the whole state into a self-management regime, with the help of the commune. Instead, the state, with the help of the commune, transformed the 'parish' into a predominantly state organisation, thereby eliminating the 'parish' as the real institution of local administration.

The net effect of the communal system is that in Yugoslavia there is neither local self-management with the classical parish as its main institution, nor competent state administration in the field. The existing commune cannot function satisfactorily as a state apparatus, for it is too amateurish, too chaotic and voluntaristic, insufficiently co-ordinated with higher administration, and not responsible enough for the execution of important duties. Without the reintroduction of local self-management based on the classical 'parish', it is impossible to imagine local government working in Yugoslavia.

Self-management in public administration

In accordance with the ideology of the Yugoslav party, the self-management system was not only supposed to operate in the economy and in local territorial communities, but also in public administration, that is at state level itself. Self-management was meant to be the general legitimate type of administration for all public spheres, as well as for the state. Yugoslavia was supposed to be a nation of 'integral' self-management. The system of self-management 'attacked' the nation with the attempt to achieve the 'self-management transformation' of a considerable part of public admin-istration.

This 'transformation' was also ideologically backed by Marxist doctrine about the 'withering away of the state'. The essence of this philosophical doctrine is the denial of the state's eternal and absolute significance. According to this doctrine, the state arose under particular circumstances as the product of the class division of society aimed at limiting social con-flicts, and as the repressive apparatus of the governing social class, it maintains public order. With the elimination of class differences, the state, it was supposed, would lose its meaning and therefore wither away. On this philosophical premise, Yugoslav political practice was con-sciously, and systematically, aimed at reducing the importance of the state through the process of 'de-etatisation'.

'De-etatisation' is the process by which certain state duties are passed on to self-management organisations, or whereby a state organ is trans-formed into an independent self-managed organisation. With the denationalistation of part of the state duties, it was expected there would be a reduction of the danger of the bureaucratisation of the socialist sys-tem of government advocated by Lenin and many other ideologists.

'De-etatisation' in state administration started after 1955, and ended with the introduction of self-management interest communities during the period 1970–80. Throughout this process all productive activities that bore any relationship to the term 'public services', in the European legal system, were denationalised and transferred to the self-management regime. Such services fall into two categories: social services such as edu-cation, culture, science, health, veterinary medicine, and social security; and material infrastructure such as transport, postal and telecommuni-cations services, railways, water services, energy, and municipal activities.

The 'de-etatisation' activities are conducted along similar lines to the economic activities, i.e. by the same type of self-management (workers' councils), and with the same means of financial and technical adminis-tration. In this framework there was always an obvious tendency to unify both kinds of activities as much as possible. With this 'de-etatisation' the size of state duties was minimised considerably, particularly at the republic and commune levels. At these levels, state duties were restricted to legal regulation and to the formulation of general guidelines for development plans.

This de-etatisation, however, was not as simple and (in principle) with-out problems, unlike the denationalisation of the economy. After 'denationalisation', the economy could at last 'breathe' independently, since it was then able to create its own income and finance itself. The above-mentioned national activities, on the other hand, could not finance themselves. It was necessary to invent a special system of financing for them, and this was the 'free labour exchange'. Similarly, it eventually turned out that is was impossible to run these organisations separately without a certain amount of co-ordination at a higher level. This role was supposed to be taken over by the newly formed 'self-management interest communities', instead of the state. These were the two major institutions which were expected to realise self-management in the 'de-etatised' areas of public administration.

The idea of free labour exchange also comes from Marx's arsenal of ideological concepts. It was intended to be the system of exchange in the future communist regime when—due to great material abundance—there would be no further need for the market exchange of goods. Rather, people would freely satisfy their own needs.

Obviously, this system could not be of such great importance in Yugoslavia. It would, however, provide a means of exchange in the 'de-etatised' spheres of state administration, which were neither a market based on equivalent exchange between partners, nor a budget based on state authority.

Free labour exchange was supposed to be based on negotiation between partners, i.e. between the 'consumers and executors' of public services such as schools, medical facilities, municipal services, etc. The consumers are individuals and enterprises, while the executors are the schools, hospitals, welfare institutions, etc. In this exchange, the negotiator is not the state and its budget, but the self-management interest community. Revenue is not collected in the form of taxes, but in the form of contributions from the income of enterprises and from the salaries of employees. Particular institutions—schools, hospitals, etc.—receive funds for their activities from self-management interest communities as payment for their services and not as budget subsidies from the state. The whole mechanism of free labour exchange was supposed to reflect self-management, not state characteristics.

In the same way as free labour exchange was supposed to replace national budget financing, i.e. instead of the state as the financier in the denationalised industries, self-management interest communities were expected to replace the state as the administrative mechanism in those areas. Self-management interest communities were created separately for each activity at both the republic and 'commune' levels, resulting in a total of several thousand. They were not conceived as special organisational institutions. Edvard Kardelj mentions only 'meetings' between the consumers and executors, who, through informal negotiations, would agree on the programmes of individual activities and the funds required for their financing. Such meetings would replace state action in these areas.

The mechanism of the free labour exchange and self-management interest communities lasted for almost two decades. It did not function as it had been conceived, i.e. managing itself independently of the state. The mechanism functioned satisfactorily, to a certain extent, only with constant state intervention. It operated with tremendous disfunctions—in the 'de-etatised' activities themselves, to the consumers of services, to society as a whole, and particularly to the public financing system.

The free labour exchange system worked as some kind of deformed budget system, backed up by the state with its might. There prevailed a legally enforceable 'principle' that one had to pay one's contributions irrespective of whether individual consumers had signed any agreement on those contributions. At the same time, the process of negotiation and the self-management mechanism themselves consumed a large proportion of the funds that were intended for the basic activities, which led to the deprivation of these activities. The self-management interest communities developed into formal institutions with an extensive organisational structure which included professional, administrative, and technical services. This resulted in the organisational and administrative duplication of state administration—as well as the self-management interest communities—with hazily defined authority and vaguely stated responsibility.

Instead of direct self-management, there was an enormously extended bureaucratisation of the system, the financing of which overloaded the economy and the population. The greatest disfunction was exemplified in the lack of control over these spheres. Since each self-management interest community carried out its own development and financial policy, co-ordination at government level was rendered difficult. The result was the overestimation of the capacities of particular activities (e.g. schools), and also great stagnation in the development of other activities, such as railways, roads, and municipal services.

Today, this segment of the Yugoslav self-management system is also ideologically dead and is in gradual liquidation. The attempt failed, leaving behind tremendous damage. The government is once again assuming its duties in these administrative spheres, as is expected of a modern state.

Conclusions

In 1945, Yugoslavia was reinstated as a socialist state of the Soviet type, i.e. as a totalitarian state which directly administered all public activities both economic and non-economic.

After the conflict with the 'Inform Bureau' in 1948, Yugoslavia started to distance itself from Soviet influence and also from the Soviet model of state administration. While searching for a different type of socialist state administration, the idea of self-management was adopted as one that would limit the state and prevent the bureaucratisation of the system, which was already evident in the state apparatus of the time. Self-management, it was thought, would reactivate the creative initiative of the people, which had begun to die away. The concept of self-management was put at the highest level of the values upon which further development of the Yugoslav system would be founded. The whole structure of Yugoslav society was intended to be based on this concept. Yugoslavia had become a society of self-management socialism.

In practice, the idea of self-management was realised in three big social complexes: the economy, local communities and public administration. The most important complex is represented by self-management in the economy, for the realisation of the whole project mostly depended on its outcome in this field. This was an original social experiment which aroused interest even outside Yugoslavia.

The second self-management complex, i.e. self-management in local communities, which took the form of a communal system, was not objectively of great importance, as it offered only an alternative to existing self-management systems in local communities in other parts of the world. Together with the third complex of self-management in public administration, however, it represented an attempt to develop a state mechanism aimed at providing an appropriate response to the well-known socialist motto of the nineteenth century: 'from the government of the people to the management of goods'.

In this way, the concept of self-management was, right from the start, one of the high-priority political and revolutionary goals. As such, its organisation and technical operation remained in the domain of politics. Self-management, like socialism, was considered as a gift from the party to the nation, which, *ipso facto*, could not be criticised. As a matter of fact, the whole execution of self-management solutions took place in the political sphere without sufficient collaboration of professionals. The revolutionary party has no trust in professionals, for it is always suspicious of their dishonest intentions, as opposed to those of the party.

Thus we may understand the numerous and serious disfunctions that were incorporated in the mechanism of self-management in the three complexes presented in this study. While the party neither saw nor wanted to see these disfunctions, the experts did not have sufficient say in the matter, either at the beginning or later. The questions arises, nevertheless, of how the party managed to be blind to some obvious imperfections in self-management, as a result of which the system could not function or functioned only with the constant external intervention of state and party officials.

One school of thought feels that the Yugoslav political leadership which conceived and devised such a system of self-management, was just a victim of Marxian ideas of the simplicity of public administration (and all other administration). These are ideas that have been around in history from the socialist utopias of the nineteenth century (the ideas of Saint-Simon, Proudhon, etc.) to Marx, who, with the analysis of the Paris Commune in 1871, developed the idea of the commune which directly manages itself without any special adminsitrative mechanism; and to Lenin who made the famous statement, 'any housewife can manage public adminis- tration.'

The fact is that all revolutionaries of the Soviet type, who organised their states according to the Soviet model, underestimated administration and did not recognise it as a special professional activity. According to them, decision-making on vital social issues is the duty of the party, while the implementation of the decisions is the job of the dependent bureau- cracy.

The other school of thought believes that the self-management system was consciously conceived and devised not to function independently, but in the presence and with the help of the state and the party. In this way, no activity would take place without the involvement of these two factors. Despite the self-management system, the state would still have everything under control, while the party would permanently justify and maintain its leading role. It would be obvious that without the party, society just could not exist. Thus, the self-management mechanism, by its very nature, would not be able to function independently.

A combination of both schools of thought is also feasible. That is, ignor- ance on the one hand—conditioned by dogmatic captivity by anachronistic ideology—and the wish on the other hand, that the monopolistic party maintain its constitutionally guaranteed leading role in society.

It has been established today that the Yugoslav attempt at creating a society of self-management socialism, whose focal point would be repre- sented by the self-managed economy, has failed miserably. We do not, however, contend that it has been proved that the effort could never have succeeded due to its basically unrealistic theoretical basis. It failed because of the enormous disfunctions which were incorporated in the mechanism of self-management, either as a result of amateurism on the part of the authors, or of the abuse of the idea of self-management, con- cealed in the desire to maintain the authority of the monopolistic party. Together with this failure, the idea of self-management itself suffered a great fiasco, at least within Yugoslavia.

In my opinion, however, the self-management concept will survive in Yugoslavia, because it is older than this unsuccessful project. Self-man- agement has proved its own lasting force through the centuries in several other countries. No doubt, its value will be proved yet in Yugoslavia, especially in local government.

3 CHARACTERISTICS, LIMITS AND PERSPECTIVES OF SELF-GOVERNMENT: A CRITICAL REASSESSMENT

Zagorka Golubović

Introduction

To set out an analysis of self-government one should begin with the following definition: 'Those performing work should be granted rights to conduct and control the conditions and results of their work performance, which requires their participation in decision-making on issues of great concern, including both the production process and social policy.'

For the historical perspective, two models of self-government can be distinguished: one which traces a line back to Proudhon, and the other following in Gramcsi's footsteps. Distrubution is the focus of the former. The main concern of the workers' councils is a just distribution of income through the market economy, harmonising a moral right with economic laws and making it possible for liberty, equality and co-operation to guarantee a fair distribution.[1] It is the market, not the factory, which is a central institution of a society organised on such a concept of self-government. The opposite perspective results from Gramsci's conception. According to this, self-government is conceived as a model of a new 'political state', in which citizens have the status of producers. This implies that factory councils serve both economic and political functions (planning and law-making).[2] The main concern thus focuses on production, and the factory is seen as the principal institution. Structurally it is a network of workers' councils linked along the line of production on the district/city/regional scale which forms the basis of self-government in Gramsci's view. It constitutes an integral 'democracy of councils' in the total social structure.

While the latter was mainly displayed in the practice of the factory committees in the Soviet Union before they were abolished (in 1918), and was an ideological inspiration of the 1918 Hungarian revolution, the Yugoslav model of self-management was primarily inspired by Proudhon's conception. This will be analysed in more detail later on. However, both models fall short when separating production from distribution, and treat them as a single dimension. The above definition incorporates both dimensions, based upon the concept of 'free associations of producers' as the agents of work activities.

The next issue concerns the requirements which should be met in order that 'free associations of producers' may be created, thus enabling a society to function under self-government. The following conditions are necessary for the basis of a self-governing organisation of society:

1. An institutional network of self-governing bodies from the grass-roots level of a regional/federal level needs to be set up, bringing together workers' councils along the production/work line. This involves a necessary structural change to the existing hierarchical/bureaucratic structure of power and management.
2. However, when following the production/work line, I do not imply that economic democracy alone (participation in production/work process) is sufficient. The latter should go in parallel with political democracy in regard to both producers' participation as citizens in decision-making where the general public is concerned, and the involvement of the councils in policy-making at all levels of society.
3. Structural change must affect the very organisation of work, first of all, in terms of diminishing the difference between the managers and those who do the job (producers), by abolishing the separation of decision-making from production.
4. Co-operation and solidarity of self-governing units are also necessary conditions for the functioning of self-government in order that the egoistic tendencies and isolation of small units can be prevented and a realisation of the common economic and social ends facilitated.
5. However, the fourth condition does not presuppose the rigid restriction of indiviudal initiative and possibilities of free choice, nor does it exclude alternative options, but rather encourages them without neglecting the rights and liberties of others (individuals and collectives).
6. Finally, the aim should be a developed civil society with its pluralistic structure in an underlying premise upon which the constitution of self-government is based. Which is to say, the members of a participatory democracy will have opportunities to choose freely from a variety of forms and options, self-government included, as against a single imposed model whose foundations cannot be challenged.

As a result of its implementation in Soviet-type societies, which do not meet the above requirements, particularly the last one, self-government has failed in practice and negative experiences have prevailed.

The main reason for the failure of self-government is precisely because the Soviet-type societies, Yugoslavia included, are constituted in a mono-organisational pattern with one-party rule as its backbone. This excludes a pluralistic network of public institutions and political organisations. It also implies a restriction of all social expression and organisations to a single concept, as permitted to the state/party-approved institutions, with no allowance for the pronouncement of different ideas. The concept of self-government assumes, first and foremost, a free choice among alternatives. Given the conditions of a monolithic political structure and the corresponding monolithic ideology, the latter is renounced under 'real socialism'.

It was impossible simply to inject self-government into the existing economic and political order of Soviet-type societies because self-government is incompatible with both a centralist command economy (even when this is decentralised as in Yugoslavia in accordance with a policentric statist pattern) and an oligarchic structure of political power. The political élite, however, may use self-government as an ideological façade, behind which it conceals the structure of oligarchic (bureaucratic) power while pretending to take steps towards democratisation.

The non-existence of pluralistic civil society offers a sound explanation for the lack of other necessary conditions that prevent both the constitution of a network of self-governing institutions from micro to macro-level and the more profound structural changes within the sphere of production as well as other public activities. This keeps intact the separation of work as execution from the planning/organisation of work activities. The result is a blockade of both conceptualisation of alternative types of self-governing organisation and their possible implementation in practice.

Industrial democracy

Another source of limitation of economic democracy in terms of workers' participation comes from a unilateral concept of industrialisation and 'technological revolution' inherent in the theory of contemporary (European) civilisation. The idea of self-government as a participatory democracy assumes, as already mentioned, harmonisation of different work dimensions which have been separated in the division of manual labour and intellectual activities. The industrial and technical civilisation fixes a limit to the abolition of the separation between work dimensions. The former is based on a presumption of the necessity for an unlimited increase of productivity and technical development which multiplies goods for consumption as an end in itself. The latter requires a further fragmentation of work and a strict determination of social roles which divides managers and planners from labourers. Hence labour consists simply of the routine and technical operations necessary for the functioning of a profitable efficient economy of commodity production. That is to say, the very concept of the modern economy, relying upon ever-increasing commodity (production which disregards both ecological problems and social/psychological consequences), contradicts the basic requirements of self-government. The latter, however, presupposes a democratic participation of individuals in all phases of production process, i.e. in planning, organisation and performance/ implementation, as well as in the distribution of the products.

On the other hand, industrial society as it prevails in our civilisation is based on the opposite assumptions, which can be expressed by a slogan such as 'the more fixed the division of labour in terms of separation of intellectual from technical skills, the better for commodity production.' Furthermore, 'industrial democracy' is grounded on a premise that the existing division of labour is justifiable from the point of view of economic efficiency, and so is a reduction of the workers' role in the performance (execution) of the job, thus hindering their participation in decision-making that concerns production in its entirety. In order to enable industrial developments to continue, irrespective of the growing dissatisfaction with the work itself, industrial societies need an authoritarian structure of power embodied in a strong state, ample evidence of which is provided in all modern societies.

A compensation for the authoritarianism which industrial/technological society requires, is gained through political democracy. This shifts emphasis on to the participation of citizens in political parties, and to the rule of law that defends citizens' (political) rights and liberties. This automatically excludes an economic democracy, which it treats as being incompatible with the requirements of industrial society and an efficient economy.

Macpherson has criticised such a restricted concept of democracy arising out of the industrial pattern of society, which reduces intelligent choices to a simple option of identifying rationality with efficiency (in technical and commodity production terms).[3] Machperson's arguments are as follows: the concept of democracy assumes a 'maximisation of human powers', hence individuals should be granted the right of using and developing their own intrinsically human attributes and capacities. Modern industrial (capitalist) society does not provide conditions for the realisation of such a concept of democracy because it legitimises the 'transfer of power' from a number of individuals to other persons (who possess not only material means of work but social power as well). An inherent obstacle in industrial society to self-government lies in unequal access to the means that enable each individual to develop his/her own potentialities and use them in public participation. An equal and free use of the available means is a precondition of possible participation in economic and political democracy that guarantees each individual the possibility of realising his/her capabilities.

A concept which is reduced to political democracy alone loses sight of economic participation and also limits the concept of pluralism of alternatives to merely the forms of political orders, while at the same time prescribing a single option for economic growth in terms of industrial and technological developments as described above. In other words, pluralism in industrial society does not apply to the sphere of work itself as one of the fundamental existential problems upon which the entire quality of life largely depends. That is because industrial society allows a free choice only in the sphere of politics, while maintaining the workers fully dependent on the techniques which require *homo roboticus* as an ideal pattern. That is the reason why the classical liberal theory does not incorporate self-government as a democratic option: it gives the term 'democracy' a purely political connotation.

From a similar reductionist viewpoint, but from different motives, self-government was thrown out of the traditional Marxist theory as a possible alternative of a 'better society'. Marxism paid no due attention to (or even rejected) political democracy as if participation in economic management were possible irrespective of the fact that an authoritarian structure of power remained intact. However, the bolshevik tradition in the Soviet Union broke with the economic democracy when discontinuing the work of spontaneously arising factory committees in the October Revolution. This was the logical result of a totalitarian type of social organisation relying upon a command economy and an authoritarian structure of power, which necessarily excluded democracy as a concept of management/government.

The fact that all the Yugoslav post-war developments bore the stamp of the Soviet model meant that such a project of self-government could not but prove unworkable. The very project was ill-conceived: that is to say, the Yugoslav new model of self-government[4] lacked a sound foundation from the outset. There was no chance of success for a number of reasons:

1. Yugoslav society was still, and had remained so throughout the post-war history, a monolithic type of society resting upon a command-pattern government/management and a single all-encompassing ruling ideology. This implies the exclusion of basic principles of self-government such as self-determination and self-organisation, and necessarily runs counter to self-government.
2. According to the prevailing ideology, the state and the party (apparatus) were viewed as the main (if not exclusive) forces entrusted with a capacity to set in motion socialist development. Therefore, the only form of 'self-government' which fitted into this pattern was a 'paternalistic self-management' treated as an appendage of the state, not as its alternative.
3. When forced to make an innovation by introducing self-management after the split with the Soviet Union occurred, the Yugoslav leadership invented the new model in a similar (Stalinist) fashion, i.e. from above.

Thus self-management was created neither as a result of the needs expressed in a social movement, nor from a theoretical/ideological reassessment of the Soviet model, on the basis of which Yugoslav society had been shaped since 1945. Moreover, having been constructed by the same figures who had devotedly implemented the Stalinist pattern of post-war developments in Yugoslavia before 1948, the project of self-management had no chance to become anything but, by and large, an empty slogan, serving as a new legitimation in hands of those who were invested with real power.

The boundaries of both the conceptualisation and implementation of the Yugoslav model of self-management were laid by its very genesis as a 'revolution from above', contradicting the concept which implies a grass-roots origin and spontaneity. It was not by accident, or simply for terminological reasons, that the term 'self-management' replaced 'self-government', for the latter assumes an overall reconstruction of social organisation, as well as changes in the sphere of social relationships. In other words, self-government requires a deep institutional transformation and structural changes which transform the concept of government in terms of inclusion of direct democracy (workers'/citizens' participation in all fields of social activities, not merely politics) as a legitimate form, not only sharing power with the classical institutions of government, but representing public control of them as well. The term 'self-management' implies only a shop-floor level of management. It reduces structural change to merely a decentralisation of economic management (i.e. from centralised state-command economic decisions to a relative autonomy of the enterprises, primarily concerned with income distribution within a factory).

Needless to say, the latter was much more congruent with the existing structure of power, which may be kept intact while allowing the institutionalisation of self-management at micro-level. A distinguishing characteristic of self-government compared with self-management can be defined in terms of the possibility of a redistribution of bureaucratic/party power, which is not necessarily challenged by existing power-holders when the latter is in question. However, even a narrow concept of self-management, which was more or less appropriate for the shop-floor level enclosed within the factory walls, could not have been realised within the given political structure of Yugoslav society. That is the reason why incongruency between words and deeds has marked the whole period since self-management as a 'Yugoslav road to socialism' has been proclaimed.

The following are the principle characteristics of the existing political system of Yugoslavia, which contradict self-government as a model of social organisation: one-party rule with an absolute and undisputable authority of the CP whose apparatus is fused with the state; the CP, which is the main property owner, generates a monopoly of power and an overall control of social activities, whose organisation is allowed and the content approved in so far as they are proved acceptable from the point of view of the state/party apparatus. Such a concentration of power producing a mono-organisational type of society *eo ipso* excludes pluralism of expressions and actions, and recognises only one authorised centre of political commands as the sole arbiter of social, political and cultural affairs.

Not having challenged the established power structure, a restrained decentralisation simply passes sets of decisions from the centralised state authorities to the enterprises. However, even such a trend was abandoned with the 1974 Constitution which restored the statist concept of socialism when decentralisation of state power from the federal to the republican states emerged as the main focus of developmental policy. The pre-1974 experiments could have offered a chance for self-management to become a vital institution, at least at the micro-level, after experiencing certain structural changes as the first step to decentralisation in terms of democratisation of management at shop-floor level (such as the abolition of a number of federal ministries and centralised planning, as well as the introduction of workers' councils as both a form of workers' participation and control of management, etc.). The 1974 Constitution put a full stop to previous trends, over which the old structure had been in ferment. It was then in the 1970s that the 'new course' was launched, reinforcing once again the state/party ruling power as one of the basic components of the existing political structure.

However, such an inversion of 'self-managing socialism', which served as a legitimation basis for party rule during the 1950s and was modified in terms of 'market socialism' in the 1960s, into a renewed statism could not have been made possible without sustaining the basic elements of the latter by and large unchanged. The evidence shows that the power structure has remained in its nature intact, irrespective of the multiplication of the centres of power and a mystification of reality and the real relations of the given social forces which were hidden under the cover of self-management. In other words, those who seized power after the Second World War have never let it go out of their hands, but have rather manipulated the institution of self-management behind the scenes of the so-called self-managing mechanisms of decision-making in the economy. As far as political decisions were concerned, the party quite openly continued to play a decisive role, never intending to step off the throne of power. A return of the party state with the 1974 Constitution has been forcefully manifested in both economic policy and politics.

What is more, the decisions granted to the workers' councils concerned primarily distribution even in the first, more successful, phase of self-management during the 1950s. Even that was restricted to the amount of income left to the enterprises after its redistribution according to state demands, including numerous taxes and obligations towards the states, both federal and republican. The main problems of how to distribute the entire income produced by enterprises, what proportion of income is to be given to the state, what is to be set aside for investment and which investments are profitable, remained the concern of the state/party apparatus. Meanwhile the enterprises with their workers' councils were put into the position of a *fait accompli* as far as the criteria of redistribution were concerned, let alone the decisions concerning production. Statistics show that the proportions of income distribution have gradually been changed to the detriment of the enterprises' autonomy, dropping from 60:40 in the 1950s and 1960s to 30:70 during the 1970s and 1980s.[5]

A conclusion reached by McVicker fits very well into this context when he says that freedom of management over the means of production means little unless it is accompanied by freedom of decision-making about who is to rule the state which determines those limited freedoms.[6] 'The failure of workers' self-management can be seen as an unintended consequence of the wish to maintain a Party monopoly of political power combined with a move to market mechanisms which have given enterprises and their managements greater independence' is a conclusion of another author.[7]

However, having remained a mixture of market and rigid intervention,[8] the economic system in Yugoslavia could not have provided a suitable basis for real independence of the enterprises in decision-making, but simply nourished their semi-independence at the local level. Given the circumstances of the workers' unchanged wage–labour position (whose only entrepreneur was the state) what has resulted is merely a quasi-participation. Therefore, Ellen Comisso's characterisation of the late phase of the Yugoslav self-management in terms of a 'more government-heavy model of self-managing socialism' (p. 119) is a good expression of such as an abortive conception, whose product could reach only the stage of a stillborn child. For the political framework within which the Yugoslav concept of self-management has emerged can be characterised as an attempt to reconcile the unreconcilable, that is, the contradictory elements of both property relations (which are neither state nor social ownership) and the political structure (which is neither state socialism nor self-management). Such a system was called by a Yugoslav author a 'directed self-management' because it had formally or semi-formally reproduced statism behind a self-managing façade,[9] with the state and the party on a higher level.[10]

A reformulation of the concept by the leading official theoretician, Edvard Kardelj, in terms of an 'integral self-government' extending to the non-productive institutions and involving a network of new forms called 'communities of self-managing interests' changed almost nothing with regard to the effects of democratisation of an authoritarian political structure. This was because Kardelj offered the so-called integral concept of self-government within a statist framework. This was shown in particular with the strengthening of the national states in the 1970s and the multiplication of the pseudo-self-governing institutions that changed only names but continued to function as para-state bodies.

The most contradictory result arising out of the application of such a model of self-government is manifest in the effects of devolution when workers' participation as a social movement is in question. The fact is that self-management in Yugoslavia has not realised workers' energy for their voluntary participation, but, on the contrary, suppressed all the workers' free movements towards the creation of new forms of a direct democracy and independent social movements or trade-unions.[11]

It would be correct to say that self-government became an ideological smoke-screen hiding the oligarchic structure of power inherent in the nature of the Bolshevik party, of which the Yugoslav CP is an example. Paradoxically as it may seem, self-government has served as an instrument of pacification of the resistance to the official (statist bureaucratic) power structure when making the latter less transparent than was the case in other East European societies.

In other words, the concept of self-government, as it was officially conceived, could not have represented a radical challenge to 'bureaucratic socialism', nor could it inspire the necessary social reforms. Its failure was logically predictable, although the institution of self-government has had some traditional roots (in particular in Serbia), and has also left some marks on post-war developments. These were primarily psychological effects in terms of workers feeling that they are not left completely at the mercy of the state, for they regarded self-government, to a certain degree, as an institution for their own use. As a matter of fact, the existing rights of self-management, no matter how restricted, were more often than not unused, either due to manipulation of the workers' councils, or because workers themselves lost confidence in the institution of self-management.

One of the reasons for the workers' loss of confidence in self-management was the growing disintegration caused by the very concept that splits workers' councils into separate units without any internal integrative component. It has been done intentionally so as to maintain the conditions requiring the party to play an integrative role in order to unite an almost completely disintegrated working class and society.

Later on, when the ideological means, whose custodian was the party, proved insufficient, a reformatory wing within the party itself offered the market as a means of integration of the disconnected economic units. When the inconsistent practice—referring to both a 'firm-hand' policy with the leading role of the party state, and a semi-market economy—failed to produce the reintegration of a complete disunity generated by an exaggerated decentralisation, the 1974 Constitution legitimised the national states as the centres of power. They were made the highest self-governing 'communities' with the final say in decision-making. From then on the national states became the entrusted bearers of national integrity.

No wonder that the disintegrative processes did not stop there, but on the contrary intensified, contributing to the complete disintegration of the working class and the entire Yugoslav population.

The policy has almost ceased to exist, thanks to the inauguration of a programme that retreated from 'self-managing market socialism', used as a slogan in the 1960s so as to identify a market economy with self-management, to the national-statist economy using the market for as long as it suited the national bureaucracies' interest in re-establishing their own power against the federal state. Self-management was abandoned because it was no longer needed as a means of legitimation when the slogan 'defence of national interest' became the trade-mark of a 'new course'. Nationalism then fitted better with the statist aspirations of the national political élites than the ideology of self-management.

Conclusions

In drawing conclusions one may agree with the statement that 'workers' self-management was the chosen solution to the problem of political survival'[12] of the Yugoslav CP after the break with the Soviet Union and with another one stating that it was the government which 'gave' self-management to the workers,[13] i.e. that self-management was neither an initiative nor a creation of the workers themselves. Thus it becomes clear why it was necessary for the Yugoslav CP to keep self-management under full control so as to avoid its becoming an independent force which could have contributed to the destruction of the one-party dictatorship. For the same reasons self-management has remained a taboo subject, used merely as a means of ideological justification of the party policy for decades to facilitate the maintenance of the status quo.

Therefore, it was the very concept of self-government which remained both theoretically and ideologically confused, according to a report on Yugoslav self-management. The statement says that Yugoslav self-management represents a 'melting-pot' of incompatible elements such as nationalisation of the means of production, overall planning, industrial democracy, autonomy of undertaking, market competition, remuneration of workers according to production and profits, etc.[14] Secondly, the concept of self-government was reduced to economic liberalisation alone, which necessarily produced the counter-effects. Being deprived of political liberalisation, self-management in Yugoslavia was used as an obstacle to the democratisation of society rather than as its impetus.

What was intrinsically missing in the thinking of the Yugoslav project of self-government was the integral component of economic and political democracy as the foundation of a self-government-based society. This assumed the creation of an open and pluralistic society, as against a half-hearted version of self-governing rights which the party state arbitrarily granted workers but could have revoked at any time. The state/party apparatus alone decides on which form of self-government is appropriate, excluding all other options.

The primary obstacle to the implementation of self-government in Yugoslavia was the destruction of civil society and the unification of society with the state. This the Yugoslav system had in common with the other countries of 'real socialism'. While the basic principle of self-government, i.e. self-organisation, presupposes the existence of independent social institutions and organisations *vis-à-vis* the state, these conditions disappeared under 'real socialism'. This is why a restoration of civil society is needed in order to lay the basis of self-government, for it cannot be implemented without the free exercise of citizens' and producers' rights in decision-making. Rights should be enjoyed by individuals without restrictions on the organisational forms and the means for their materialisation, provided that the rights and liberties of other people are not threatened.

In other words, the right of an individual to be a citizen has to be restored in order that he/she may use civil liberties as a precondition of becoming a responsible member of a self-governing community. This assumes the need for a transformation of the state supervised by the party (a party-state) into a *Staatsrecht*—the rule of law—whose main task is to guarantee civil rights and liberties, self-governing rights included, and to defend independence of social activities and movements.

The introduction of self-government was too great a challenge to the Yugoslav educated leadership. Hence it had no choice but to compromise by offering a short-sighted version in order to come to terms with its inherited ideology. This was how a still-born child—Yugoslav self-management—arrived on the Yugoslav scene.

In looking from the above angle at the genesis of self-management in Yugoslavia and its results, the question of whether the present-day crisis of Yugoslav society was generated by self-management is misleading. The crisis is not the outcome of self-management practice, but rather of its obstructions. In fact, it was generated, but only partly, by a confused idea of self-government inserted into an inappropriate political system, itself a logical consequence of a concept of socialism which had not liberated itself from its Stalinist heritage.

Notes

1. See Ellen Comisso, *Worker's Control under Plan and Market, Implications of Yugoslav self-management*, New Haven, Yale University, 1979, pp. 23–30.
2. Ibid., pp. 4–20.
3. C.B. Macpherson, *Democratic Theory*, Oxford, Clarendon Press, 1984; see the first essay 'Maximalisation of democracy'.

4. In the official terminology, it is self-management which is in use as a Yugoslav model, although both terms are present in the official documents as interchangeable. However, it is more correct to use the former because the concept in the Yugoslav project concerns primarily management, as it will be elaborated in the following passages.
5. See Ichak Adizes, *Industrial Democracy, The Yugoslav Style*, New York, The Free Press, 1971, pp. 20–8.
6. Charles P. McVicker, *Titoism: pattern for international communism*, New York, St Martin's Press, 1957, pp. 263–4.
7. Leslie Benson, 'Market socialism and class structure: manual workers and managerial power in the Yugoslav enterprise', in Frank Parkin (ed.), *The Social Analysis of Class Structure*, London, Tavistock Publications, 1974, p. 270.
8. See Alec Nove, *The Economics of Feasible Socialism*, London, Allen and Unwin, 1983, p. 137.
9. This is the statement of a prominent Yugoslav sociologist and economist, Josip Županov, who has written a number of significant works on self-management; for instance *Selfmanagement and Social Power* (Samoupravljanje i društvena moć), Zagreb, Globus, 1985.
10. See F. Singleton, *Twentieth Century Yugoslavia*, London, Macmillan, 1976, p. 312.
11. See A. Meister, *Où va l'autogestion Yugoslave?*, Paris, Edition Anthropos, 1970, p. 329.
12. See John H. Moore, *Growth with Self-Management, Yugoslav Industrialisation, 1952–1975*, Stanford, California, Hoover Institute Press, 1980, p. 4.
13. A. Meister, op. cit., p. 87.
14. *Worker's Management in Yugoslavia* (Reports), International Labour Office, Geneva, 1962, pp. 294–5.

Select bibliography

Adizes, I., 1971. *Industrial Democracy, The Yugoslav Style*, New York, The Free Press.

Benson, L., 1974. 'Market Socialism and Class Structure: manual workers and managerial power in the Yugoslav enterprise', in Frank Parkin (ed.), *The Social Analysis of Class Structure*, London, Tavistock Publications.

Yugoslav self-management, New Haven, Yale University Press.

Golubović, Z. and Stojanović, S., 1986. *The Crisis of the Yugoslav System*, in the series 'Crisis in the Soviet-Type System', Study no. 14, Munich.

Horvat, B., Marković, M. and Supek, R. (eds.), 1976. *Selfgoverning Socialism*, New York, International Arts and Science Press.

Rusinov, D., 1977. *The Yugoslav Experiment 1948–1974*, London, Hurst.

Singleton, F., 1985. *A Short History of the Yugoslav Peoples*. Cambridge University Press.

Wachtel, H.M., 1973. *Workers' Management and Workers' Wages in Yugoslavia: the theory and practice of participatory socialism*, Ithaca, Cornell University Press.

4 FROM THE NEW SOCIAL MOVEMENTS TO POLITICAL PARTIES

Tomaž Mastnak

Introduction

At the beginning there was punk. Only later we named it the first new social movement (NSM) in this country.[1] When it emerged in 1977, it was a youth subculture. Looking back we understand it as the first attempt to build an independent society. It anticipated the future. When it first appeared, there was 'no future'. In the early 1970s, Tito and his 'soldiers of the revolution' (as the orthodox Communists used to call themselves) suppressed, by a nationwide massive purge of economic, political and cultural apparatuses, the liberalisation of the country. The 1970s were then the era of cultural revolution. The punk in Slovenia was the first breach of this settlement.

'The Children of Socialism' was the name of a punk band. Protagonists of the movement, however, were the first generation free from socialist ideology. They renamed the world they lived in and created new cultural codes, *altri codici*, to use Melucci's term. Their confrontation with the system, if confrontation at all, was already a confrontation from outside. They mocked it, made fun of it, rather than criticise it seriously; and when they took it seriously it was only to imitate it, and in this way display its totalitarian mechanisms. Their declared hedonism was as subversive to the misanthropic ascetic ethics of the communist regime as their analysis was to its social and political imagery. As ideology is the symbolic bond that holds society together, this first dissolution of socialist ideology somehow unbounded the society. One could not expect, however, that the reaction of the authorities would be an ideological one, it was police repression. Yet it failed, and its failure set the terms for the developments in the 1980s. I shall (1) describe this conflict (which took place in 1980–1); and then proceed to (2) the emergence of other NSMs and the formation of independent social spheres (one could term this period from the late 1970s to the mid-1980s the rediscovery of civil society); and to (3) the growing politicisation of independent social activities (the late 1980s).

The punk question

There are three main reasons for the failure of the system to solve the 'punk question' with the use of police force and violence.[2] First, there was the intelligence of the protagonists of the punk scene and their ability to enforce public discussion on the accusations invented by the police and disseminated by mass media. The conflict was displaced from the repressive to the ideological level. Two other conditions had to be fulfilled in order to make this displacement work. Second, for the first time after the decade of intensified communist dictatorial rule (if not after the end of the war which textbooks have called 'liberation' *tout court*), the ideological and political divisions carefully cultivated by the power to split (critical) intelligence and fragment society were overcome and there was a broader mobilization of independent public. This 'democratic front' refuted the use of violence to solve social problems in general and the 'anti-youth chauvinism' of the authorities in particular. Third, the official youth organisation (ZSMS) gave in to the pressure 'from below', i.e. it ventured contacts with the critical and active segment of the young generation aggregated around the punk scene to listen to its arguments. It made a public discussion possible in which all concerned could take part; and instead of acting as an executive body following the police instructions, it demanded evidence from the police (of course, it had no evidence to justify the repression). This was without precedent.

An English reader might wonder what is so exceptional about it all. In order to offer an explanation I must sketch briefly some characteristic features of the socialist system. First of all, under socialism there is no place for autonomous social activities or independent social spheres. Socialism excludes the very notion of independent society. Punk in Slovenia not only proved that independent social life was possible, moreover, it invented the concept itself, it created elements for the formation of a new social and political language. Further, under socialism there is no public sphere, properly speaking, let alone an independent public. The place where it should be is occupied by party-state ideological apparatuses. They are producing an immense amount of written and spoken material not to encourage the subjects ('citizens' were eliminated as a 'bourgeois' category) but to prevent them from speaking or writing themselves. A substitute for public discussion is the display of the so-called intellectual life of the party, a public discussion as such is always a scandal. Political organizations—the party and its transmissions—exist to aggregate compulsorily people who have been deprived of the freedom to associate politically.[3] They do not have members, they take prisoners. It is not their aim to mediate for their social interests or represent them in decision-making, but to disarticulate them. Finally, the police—especially the state security— are the stronghold of the regime, in the 'best' case responsible only to the highest party-state leaders; they are the source of their knowledge and the executor of their will. Under the rule of *securitate* there is no legal security.

To summarise, punk was a 'symbolic challenge' (see Melucci 1985), not a real threat. Yet it had far-reaching consequences and has made this experience so important. The first NSM in Slovenia conceived politics as symbolic action. It opposed this reinvention of the modern democratic notion of politics[4] to the system in which political power was understood as a real thing. In this way, it challenged the very nature of the socialist system.

New social movements

The failure of the attempt to repress the punk movement opened the way for autonomous social activities. In fact, in the years that followed new NSMs emerged in Slovenia: pacifist, environmentalist, feminist, gay, spiritual ('new age') . . . By the mid-1980s a network of NSM and youth subcultures was formed which perceived itself as the 'alternative scene' or simply the 'alternative'. The actors were mainly young people under 18, which points to the fact that the cultural revolution had successfully devastated the university—almost no students were involved. On the other hand, younger intellectuals who had finished their studies in the 1970s played an important role. Some of the most able among them (many of whom could not find work in the university as they were declared 'morally–politically inappropriate'[5]) found their way to and their place in the alternative scene. Their great concern was to avoid the dangers of vanguardism. They became a group among other groups, and the most propulsive political and social theory a part of the alternative culture. This constellation contributed to a permanent reflection of the alternative and to its clear understanding of the social and political 'environment'; besides this, the intellectuals had the skills to refute ideological and political attacks on the scene and to preserve the space for its other protagonists to articulate themselves.

A crucial role in the formation of the alternative scene was played by the local radio station, Ljubljana-based *Radio Student* (Radio Student). Its programme linked the broadcasting of music, mainly rock'n'roll, to political analysis and theoretical discourses. Out of this mixture of youth subcultures, criticism of Stalinism/communism/socialism/totalitarianism, 'post-Marxism' and Lacanian psychoanalysis—to which very soon particular issues put forward by pacifists and anti-militarists, gays, feminists and ecologists were added—sprang the new political culture. The importance of *Radio Student* created a subtle sense of media, which was important in two respects: it led to the formation of alternative media and it helped to define effective tactics and strategies in dealing with the established, or official, media. The first independent publications (leaflets, fanzines, bulletins, records, tapes, books, video) appeared in the alternative, yet this was only a part of the formation of alternative media. Not less decisive were the attempts to influence or take over the official media. The important aspect of this strategy was that these attempts originated in an already existing alternative public sphere, and are to be understood as its expansion (which implies that the alternative public sphere cannot be regarded as a refuge of those who failed, for whatever reasons, in the official media). The greatest success in this respect was the transformation of the ZSMS weekly *Mladina* (The Youth), which in the mid-1980s became the forum of the independent society and soon after the most influential political magazine in the country. Some other—similarly marginal—media changed as well. The central media, however, resisted the new developments and remained closed to the new ideas. This meant that the editors-in-chief remained loyal servants to the power-holders by whom they had been appointed, which caused great discontent among journalists. A number of them organised and declared themselves bound by professional ethics and not by the party line.[6] In the mid-1980s the official media monolith began to crumble.

To complete this outline of how the independent public sphere took shape, I have to mention two more movements. Intellectuals of the mid-generation, more or less established yet critical of the existing system and dissatisfied with their role in it, succeeded in founding an independent journal, *Nova revija* (The New Journal), which was to become one of the most influential oppositionalist publications. On the other hand, professional organisations—like those of writers (close to *Nova revija*), sociologists and philosophers—reactivated themselves and became involved in this 'rebirth' of society. Soon some of the academic institutions outside the university joined this movement, too.

Civil society

The concept that summarised all these phenomena and developments was that of a 'civil society'. However long the history of the concept may be, it was rediscovered, or rather reinvented, in 1983. Roughly speaking, civil society was understood as a sphere distinct from, independent of and opposed to the sphere of the state action, and as such it was perceived as the alternative to the socialist system. This needs explanation.

Firstly, out of the elements which contributed to the reinvention of civil society, the following should be mentioned:

1. The state–civil society distinction was experienced by the Slovene punk, and later alternative, scene. It was the police repression and 'legal' persecution[7] of its protagonists which highlighted this distinction most clearly.
2. The Solidarity movement in Poland enjoyed great sympathy, and support as well.[8] The programmatic discussions of the Czech and Hungarian democratic opposition were presented a little later.
3. Contacts were made with the 'post-marxist' discussions on civil society in the West.[9]

Second, civil society as the alternative was invented by the alternative, and the concept was first applied to its inventor, as an analytical model and political norm. The actors of the alternative scene—NSM in the first instance—were understood to be the main actors in the constitution of civil society; its institutions as the crucial institutions of the civil society in formation; and the alternative public sphere as the catalyst of the independent public.

Third, something has to be said on the contents of the concept. It is true that its first articulation was the 'socialist civil society', only to find out that the concept of civil society is incompatible with the idea of socialism and its reality. The state–civil society distinction offered the starting-point to refute self-management as an anti-statist and anti-social project. By abolishing the difference between the state and civil society, it withered away the state as well as civil society. This created an amorphous system which synthesised a powerless, yet omnipresent and irresistible domination and a powerful, yet flabby, voluntary servitude (to use an old La Boétie concept). As such, self-management—as the idea(l) and as the reality—was a deformed creature, Leviathan and Behemoth at the same time.

The reinvention of civil society, in the given case, was a rediscovery of democracy against the idea of democratic socialism. Civil society, distinct from the state and opposed to any idea of harmonious community, was conceived as the necessary condition for democracy; and practical steps towards reaffirming the distinction and thereby constituting a 'real existing' civil society and a proper state—possibly a *Rechtsstaat*—were regarded as a process of democratisation. This also implied that direct democracy models became undesirable. Classical liberal, or even better, the modern-democratic, ideas re-emerged to be articulated with the ethos of NSM, with the postmodern democratic experiences.

The struggle for legitimation

There were, in that period, no possibilities for NSM to register to gain a legal status which would, to a certain degree, protect them against arbitrary state repression. A solution was found in making a kind of contract with ZSMS. NSM formally became attached collective members of ZSMS without giving up their autonomy, or, if we look at it from the other side, ZSMS became an umbrella organisation for those movements, groups and initiatives. Both partners had their benefits. NSM gained legality and ZSMS acquired a growing legitimacy. I do not interpret this symbiosis as an attempt to integrate NSM in the system or as a form of surveillance, but rather as a decisive step towards transforming the system. On the one hand, the very existence of NSM meant introducing pluralism: not only were there other subjects than the party and its replicants on the scene, but also, new forms of activity, new forms of organisation, were invented. On the other hand, looking for legitimacy already meant renouncing the principle of communist dictatorship (a rule based on acclamation obtained by force and without legitimacy), and the same is true with regard to tolerating or even protecting any form of autonomous activity.

Yet this new constellation only caused the restructuring of repression against the key actors of independent society, and civil society proved to be an ambiguous phenomenon. If civil society is a necessary condition of democracy, it is not necessarily democratic itself. If there is no democracy without civil society, it is still not impossible to imagine civil society without, or acting against, democracy. This is what happened in Slovenia in the first half of the 1980s.

The attempt to eliminate the emerging network of NSM with repressive state intervention failed, for the civil society organised around this network succeeded in (1) pushing the state repression into legal framework; and (2) imposing rational terms of discourse in the public debate on the issue. Consequently, carrying on the repression would have been perceived as an open violation of laws, while its advocates would only have made themselves ridiculous by justifying it with party–state ideological hallucinations. At that point, the state gave up repression and handed it over to civil society. The social violence concentrated in the state (to allude to a Marxian formula) was dispersed and given back to society; or, the state transferred part of its authority to civil society: the violence was socialised and the state partially withered away.

What had been state violence ceased to be political as soon as civil society interiorised it. Previously directed agains the protagonists of the alternative scene personally, it now turned against the appearances of the otherness in public and aimed at elimination of the social spaces of difference and otherness. Places specially designed for production and/or consumption of alternative culture were closed down one after another, and it became increasingly difficult to rent places for performances. The alternative population was thus fragmented and took refuge in bars, coffee-houses or restaurants, only to be driven away again (the places were closed down, reconstructed, an entrance fee was imposed, their purpose was redefined, the personnel refused to serve punks and other unconventional clients, and so on). It was forced constantly to migrate, and after each migration it grew smaller, it became more fragmented and demoralised. The symbolic presence of the alternative in the city was systematically eradicated, graffiti writers persecuted, graffiti erased, posters and notices torn down, etc.[10] All these oppressive and repressive activities were clearly unpolitical and unplanned; nobody 'in the background' pulled the strings; it was all grass roots. Reasons for closing down the places were of a technical nature—urbanistic, traffic, hygienic, fire-preventative, earthquake-preventative, sound-proof isolation, etc. All and everything was initiated, put into practice and executed by the people themselves, hating those who look and behave differently, fearing AIDS, demanding quiet at night, complaining about urinating at corners, etc. They acted in the name of the moral majority or as the *vox populi* instigating 'the responsible' to assume measures. They organised themselves as residents in neighbourhoods, as citizens in the local communities, as 'social owners' of the public places or as workers in the coffee-houses. They were the socialist consciousness and the nation's conscience synthesised. The attempted elimination of the social spaces of difference and otherness was an experience in 'direct democracy'. Civil society turned up against its own democratic potentials. I call this phenomenon totalitarianism from below.

Totalitarianism from below

Totalitarianism from below could not gain the upper hand yet it has remained present as a feature of the rediscovered civil society which has to be taken into account. If it could not eliminate NSM, this does not mean it has not influenced their development. It has had an impact on general developments as well. In the mid-1980s the first major differentiation in the NSM network, or in the alternative scene, occurred; it was also the time when the modernisation of the system started. I shall first concentrate on the former aspect.

Due mainly to totalitarianism from below, parts of independent social activities excluded themselves from the public, from the communicative exchange in 'society at large'. They gave up their striving to speak publicly and expectations to be listened to; they ceased to refer to public discussions and common values; they chose speechlessness[11] as their language to communicate with 'society'. In this respect they decided to be silent but refused to be silenced. They did not give up their activity, they just turned it inwards and dedicated it to themselves. Far from having to deal with a kind of quietism, we have to recognise a new logic of social activities. We have to deal with social activities which do not need an external adversary to constitute themselves, and which, in their practice, therefore do not seek to negate the adversary's position, but rather grapple with their own internal lacks and auto-blockades, with their own barriers and insufficiencies, which work on their own limits and limitations, and which live their impossibility. I described them as the implosion of the social.[12]

On the other hand—contrary to this silent and invisible, imploded, civil society—totalitarianism from below, reactions to it and its only partial success led to an explosion of the social. Civil society definitively reappeared. The resistance to the attempt to eradicate the social spaces of difference and otherness, to eradicate differences and otherness from the social, initiated or intensified the struggle of the major part of NSM for their presence in the public. They oriented their activities to the public, presenting their programmes, ideas and concrete initiatives, reacting to the slander or accusations against them. In the mid-1980s, first, independent demonstrations were organised, numerous petitions, open letters and public statements written, a number of seminars held, feminists appeared in public, homosexuals organised the first week of gay culture in Ljubljana in 1984, etc. The major success in popularising NSM ideas, however, was the peace movement's initiative for the recognition of conscientious objection and the introduction of a civilian service as the alternative to the military service.[13] It was furiously attacked by the army and—mainly federal or Serbian—political bodies, and it has not disappeared from mass media for years.[14] The idea became known, and along with it other ideas forming the social and political imagery of NSM. The greater part of Slovene society has accepted them.

What happened might be explained with the help of Kant's interpretation of the French Revolution. Kant, as it is well known, saw the greatness of the revolution not in the event itself (in the revolutionary drama), but in the feelings of enthusiasm it aroused in those who were not directly involved, who were spectators of the historic spectacle.

The revolution of the witty nation which has been taking place in these days before our eyes might succeed or fail; it might be the cause of such a misery and such atrocities that a well-intentioned man, was he in position which would give hope to accomplish it successfully for a second time, would never take the decision to make the experiment at such a price—what I am saying is that this revolution invokes in the sentiments of all the spectators (who themselves are not involved in the play) the desire *to participate* which borders nearly to enthusiasm and the expression of which meant to take a risk, the cause of which could therefore be only a moral disposition in the human race.[15]

Kant recognised in this willingness, or desire, to participate—the *signum*

rememorativum, demonstrativum, prognosticon, i.e. the historical sign that
testifies to the fact that humanity is progressing to the good. NSMs under
socialism, or more exactly, the enthusiasm they provoked in the people
not directly involved, were such a *signum rememorativum, demonstrativum,
prognosticon*.[16]

Communist party loss of the youth

In 1985, the term civil society first appeared in the discourse of the ruling
party. This was a symptom of the Slovene League of Communists' (ZKS)
changing attitude to the new reality. After the repression failed, they
ignored NSM, hoping they were only a fashionable aping of the Western
counterparts which would soon pass. They had to learn it was a vain hope.
So they began to look for ways to catch hold of the new concepts and
thereby to disarticulate NSM. On the one hand, they tried to reintegrate civil
society into Marxist political language, to interpret it with a help of
Gramscian neo-Marxism, in order to prove that civil social issues are
'organically' or 'essentially' linked to the existing self-management project,
that this model is in fact the genuine civil society coming true and that
civil society in that sense is in fact the party's programmatic aim. On the
other hand, they proceeded with an ideological 'differentiation' of NSM,
recognising them, in principle, as an understandable and positive phenomenon, yet refuting as negative features all that which was new about them,
critical of the system or subversive to it: in short, all that would escape
integration and pacification. NSMs were good, only their actors, ideas,
actions and aims were unacceptable. Anyway, it took some years for these
ideas to take form. By that time, the party had to realise it had not to compete for a concept but to 'struggle for the youth' (according to the party
plenum in 1987). When it launched this struggle, however, the loss of the
youth to its politics was already a *fait accompli*.

An event of decisive importance in that period was the ZSMS congress
in 1986.[17] Quite unexpectedly, ZSMS departed radically and definitively
from the role of a 'youth transmission party' designed for it by the party-
state. It declared itself to be an organisation in civil society based on the
achieved level of social self-organisaion, which was understood to be the
only real basis of democratisation of the country. It ceased to be the
umbrella organisation of NSMs. It adopted the issues put on the agenda
by NSMs without destroying their autonomy. It transformed itself to enable
closer collaboration with the movements and initiatives and more effective
dealing with concrete problems. The alternative scene achieved in this
way its counterpart in the political system.

The end of the political monolith, the loss of the youth to the official
politics and relatively strong and clearly articulated civil society com-

pelled the party and its replicants to take steps towards reforms. On the one hand, the party gradually eliminated the 'old guard' and cautiously started its process of transformation to a social democratic party. On the other hand, the Socialist Alliance of Working People (SZDL), a 'crypto'-communist popular front organisation, tried to integrate independent social groupings, offering them legitimacy if they agreed to work under its umbrella.

The relay of youth

In 1987, Tito died symbolically. It was his second and final death. ZSMS proposed to put an end to the 'relay of youth'. This was a ritual in the best tradition of the socialist-realist mass manifestations. Young people all over the country had to carry around a phallic symbol which was finally handed over to 'our dearest Marshal Tito', with a letter in it swearing to the leader the eternal loyalty of the young generation to the legacy of the 'liberation struggle', to their Yugoslav fatherland and communism. This running around with a stick, which was meant to symbolise 'brotherhood and unity', was heavily loaded with militarist spirit and it logically ended each year at the stadium of the Yugoslav People's Army (JNA) in Belgrade: thousands of disciplined young bodies lying on the ground at Tito's feet. The ritual was not given up when Tito died which only underlined its absurdity. As the proposal was rejected, ZSMS refused to take part. When it was compelled to participate, it tried to deconstruct the ritual from within. Among other things, a group of young artists called *Neue slowenische Kunst*, long persecuted by the Slovene authorities, designed a poster for the event, which was a remake of an old Nazi poster. The federal organisational committee was happy to accept it—it obviously found that the poster expressed the spirit of the 'relay of youth' very well—only to learn about the original later. A great scandal broke out. It is true that this was the last 'relay', but a hostile campaign against the forces carrying out the democratisation in Slovenia was launched from Belgrade (it is still going on: it has only changed its forms and, partly, targets).

So the Yugoslav context of NSM took form. Movements and initiatives in Slovenia have had no proper dialogue partner in other Yugoslav republics except a pacifist, ecologist and feminist group in Zagreb (called *Svarun*) and some individuals or small *ad hoc* groups elsewhere. On the other hand, a phalanx of the *ancien régime* was formed against NSM, with JNA at its heart.

We dispose of the evidence now that the counter-intelligence service already started an operation against democratisation in Slovenia, called *Mladost* ('youth' in Serbian), in 1985. This means that the alternative scene was for years under the surveillance of the military police, whose finding it was that NSM and other autonomous activities were 'anti-socialist'. JNA and its mouthpieces became more aggressive in the spring of 1988 when Slovene newspapers criticised the scandalous Yugoslav (i.e. JNA's) arms trade,[18] and *Mladina* revealed corruption in the army (soldiers on military service had to build a private villa for the Secretary of Defence). The generals declared this to be 'attacks on JNA', and inspired the federal political authorities to make a statement that there was a 'counter-revolution' in Slovenia. This statement then in turn empowered the army to act, and early in 1988 a military intervention in Slovenia was about to take place. I must break the narrative at this point to offer a brief explanation of the role of the army.

In the first half of the 1980s, the repressive apparatuses of the state began to take over the formulation and interpretation of the official ideology, i.e. the ideology of those in power. The general reason for this shift is to be found in the fact that the 'Yugoslav model' had exhausted its potentials. This fact could be perceived much more easily as not only had the so-called crisis aggravated the situation but also the charismatic leader had gone and the spell he had upon the people began slowly to disappear. With the decline of socialism becoming obvious, the party was losing the initiative. It gradually began to dissolve[19] and ceased to be 'the leading ideological force', as the Constitution defined its role. At the trial of the 'Belgrade six', it was the public prosecutor who imposed himself as the great ideologist. As the trial turned out to be a disaster for the authorities—the same could be said for a number of trials against the editors of and contributors to *Mladina*—public prosecutors were succeeded by generals. The army obtained the position of the ideological arbiter and took possession of the right to declare what socialism means, that is, what is allowed and what is to be prosecuted.

The shift from the party to the army in the production of the official ideology was not a violent one. JNA is not only the party's army, it is itself organised as a party. The officers (predominantly Serbs) are all communists and their party's organisation is a constitutive member of the federal party. Given that the party is constructed on territorial principles (which means that the republic organisations constitute the Yugoslav League of Communists), this is an exemption from the rule. The JNA's party organisation is federal in itself and at the same time a constitutive element of the federal party organisation. As a particular political body it embodies unmediated universality and is a movement of the mediated universality of Yugoslav communism. (Structuralists would describe it as the surplus which determines the meaning and reveals the truth of the communist totality). The truth of the Communist party is the armed party. This is Marxism in its active reality. According to a well-known Marxian metaphor, ideology becomes a material force at the moment when it has gripped the masses. As the official ideology as such had begun to lose its grip on the masses, when its development into a material force had begun to fail, the armed party as material force in itself set in. Communism was reduced to its hard core—to the pure violence.

The Committee for the Defence of Human Rights

A peak of this repressive transformation of ideology was reached in the summer of 1988. An officer appeared as the public prosecutor. A military trial was held in Ljubljana. Two editors of *Mladina*, its contributor, an important figure in the opposition, and a sergeant-major of JNA, Slovene by origin, were charged with betraying a secret military document. The military court found them guilty without ever having proved the case. It was clearly a political show-trial, blatantly violating a number of laws, procedures and the Slovene constitution, which aimed at the suppression of democratisation in Slovenia. This target, however, was not reached because of an unexpectedly strong and resolute social mobilisation and resistance. The reaction of the public to the arrests and the criminal prosecution was immediate, massive and energetic. A committee for the defence of the defendants, called the Committee for the Defence of Human Rights, was founded in Ljubljana, to become the organisationsal centre of a nation-wide democratic movement. It had more than a thousand collective members, along with more than 100,000 individuals who joined it.[20] What I am interested in here is how these developments influenced NSM.

The Committee for the Defence of Human Rights was formed in a period in which a cycle of NSMs was coming to an end—they had been legalised, their ideas had become the common good and their issues a matter of public concern—and a debate started on their future. The first effect the repression and the organised resistance to it had on NSM was the suppression of this debate. The second major effect of the new constellation on NSM was that the social resistance absorbed their remaining energies. All NSMs joined the Committee and their most active protagonists began to play an important role in it. The Committee could have never had such a success and would have not become the most—indeed, the first—really massive democratic organisation in the country after the Second World War if the NSMs had not created the independent society. The Committee in fact successfully capitalised on the experience of the NSMs; these, however, had, so to speak, to suspend their 'proper' activities when this happened. In this sense, the Committee was rather the discontinuity in the 'history' of NSM as its 'higher stage'.

The Committee also caused a complex shift in the structuring of independent activities. Contrary to NSM who had pursued their positive programmes, the Committee's activity was a defensive, negative one: a reaction to

the federal state repression. The major shift, however, was that from independent social to independent political activity. Formerly unpolitical or
'anti-political'[21] autonomous activities were absorbed into politics. The
Committee unified the field of action into a political field of action. The
sphere of independent social activities somehow vanished: the emergence
of political opposition coincided with the disappearance of opposition to
politics. On the other hand, the very existence of the Committee
pluralised the political space. It represents the first real case of practising
political pluralism in the country. This was, however, a frustrated pluralism:
the political space was only bipolarised, with the Committee on the one
side and the weakening official politics on the other.

The effect of this differentiation of political space—or the price for it—
was the homogenisation of the independent sphere. This happened so
much more easily, since the threat to the democratisation in Slovenia
came from outside, from Belgrade. The defence of democracy, the nation-
wide democratic movement, assumed a nationalist form. The cause of
democracy was linked to the question of national sovereignty.

There is yet another feature of these developments. The Committee
was founded to help the defendants, the goal of its activity was purely
legalistic, unpolitical. It was this unpolitical platform which attracted and
unified its numerous individual and collective members. So it could happen that people of the most diverse political orientations joined forces and
worked together. However, the logic of the space in which the Committee
was formed and had to conduct its activities compelled it to act politically,
the political nature of these activities was imposed by the system. The
Committee became a political organisation without ever having had a
political platform. So it became a political organisation in which the members had to suppress their political identity. With regard to the NSMs this
meant that they ceased to be social movements and had to give up dealing
with their particular issues. They had lost their identity twice without
being in position to develop a political identity.

Formation of political parties

Due to the mass mobilisation structured around the Committee for
Defence of Human Rights, democratisation in Slovenia was saved. As this
became clear, the structural tensions created inside the Committee were
set free. Political identities were gradually articulated. In the autumn of
1988, the formation of political parties started. Its background was the
growing autonomy and strength of civil society, as well as its inner differentiation and pluralisation which created the need for political representation. The forces of socialist self-management resisted this process, yet
step by step they had to made concessions. As it became clear that political

pluralism was inevitable—unless one should risk a total blockade of social dynamics, which was not a viable option at the stage when the development of socialism had exhausted all the resources—they argued for a 'non-party political pluralism'. In the end, even the SZDL, the most ardent advocate of this idea, transformed itself into a party and stood for elections in the spring of 1990. The same happened to ZKS. The party transformed itself into a party and contributed considerably to a non-violent transition from totalitarianism to parliamentary democracy.

I should like to highlight three movements which, more than others, constituted this political transition. What was at stake was the question of demonopolisation of power. ZSMS declared its 'struggle for power' in 1988. It should be mentioned that the 'struggle for power' used to be the final accusation of the communist rulers—claiming to have the historical mandate to govern—against their opponents. To struggle for power was a deadly sin. When ZSMS declared it was struggling for power, this not only meant that it refused to obey 'Big Brother', it was, moreover, already a redefinition of the nature of power. ZKS, on the other hand, began to talk about its 'descent from power' more or less in the same period. It recognised its monopoly of power was generating the crisis and at the same time blocking any attempt to solve it, and was consequently a dead end; and it realized it had to share power in order not to lose it completely. What both processes, or declarations, have in common is the modern-democratic concept of power as an 'empty space'.[22] Both strategies have contributed to the constitution of democratic political space.

The third movement was a kind of round-table talks in the spring of 1989. They have their history. Already the Committee established regular contacts with the authorities. It happened that for the first time they recognised a declared oppositional organisation as their dialogue partner. The results of those contacts were relatively unsatisfying for both sides, but the ice was broken. The next event of major importance was a meeting held in Ljubljana early in 1989. In Staritrg in Kosovo, 1,300 Albanian miners were on hunger-strike deep in the pits to protest against the plan of the Serbian leadership to suspend the autonomy of the Kosovo province.[23] As the local, Serbian and federal authorities refused to talk to the miners even after the strike had been going on for a week and the lives of the strikers were seriously endangered, a group of people from the Slovene opposition decided to organise a meeting in solidarity with them and in protest against the behaviour of the political authorities. The motive was to do something to save the miners' lives. All the oppositional groups and the official political organisations in Slovenia joined this initiative and their highest representatives gave speeches at the meeting. This was the first joint political action by the oppositionalists and the officials. The Serbian leadership reacted madly, calling people on the streets and threatening that this party mob will come to Ljubljana. In order to prevent such an occupation, the protagonists of the solidarity and protest meeting in Ljubljana decided to continue meeting and to co-ordinate their activities. As the danger of the Serbian occupation passed, meetings of this co-ordinative body concentrated on the political future of Slovenia. This was the beginning of the end of the meetings, due mainly to the SZDL's ambition to keep everything in its hands.

The opposition was quasi-legalised in this way. Soon after, the law on political organisations was passed. The decision was made to arrange free elections in the spring of 1990. Five oppositional parties formed a coalition called Demos. The other coalition was formed by ZKS and SZDL. ZSMS decided to stand for election alone. At that moment, as political pluralism triumphed and parliamentary democracy was endorsed, the NSMs re-appeared. Regardless of the still good relations with ZSMS—which transformed itself into a party at its congress in the autumn of 1989 and declared itself the Liberal party soon after—protagonists of NSM recognised that no political party could deal with their issues satisfactorily. They resolved to stand for election alone, as the Independent List of NSMs. It seems that the debate on their future activity, interrupted by the military trial in 1988, will have to be resumed.

Half a year later: *ora et labora*

The former opposition is now in power and the formal heirs of the 'official political organisations' represent the opposition in the post-communist Slovene Parliament. An unknown Christian Democrat has become the Prime Minister, the leader of the Committee for Defence of Human Rights is now the Secretary for Internal Affairs, and one of the defendants of the 'Military Trial' the Secretary for Defence. The red star has disappeared from the national flag and the word 'Socialist' has been removed from the name of the Republic of Slovenia which has declared itself a sovereign nation-state.[24] This is the result of the elections: some feel it represents the historic resurrection (if not ascension) of the Nation, others understand that this is not exactly what they had strived and hoped for while fighting communism.

In the elections, Demos obtained about 55 per cent of the votes. However, the two strongest single parties in Parliament are ZKS-Party of Democratic Renewal and ZSMS-Liberal party. They are followed by Christian Democrats. This was an unpleasant surprise for the ideological core grouping of Demos, the Slovene Democratic Alliance, which had assumed they would win the elections. The results were, nevertheless, a promising starting-point to create a democratic and pluralist political system. First, the fact that Demos won with a minimal majority seemed to lessen the dangers—and temptations—of the formation of a new monopolistic power, while its victory made possible the deconstruction of the old one. Second, the Communists—the Party of Democratic Renewal—were not eliminated from political life although they had lost power. This certainly was an expression of political realism and gave the impression that *révanchisme* would not play a major role. Third, the relative electoral success of ZSMS-Liberal party meant the presence of a third political bloc (still sensitive to NSM and their issues), and consequently an element of a pluralist, not just dualist, political space.

On the basis of the electoral results one would have expected that power would be divided and shared by all the relevant political forces in the country. Demos, however, has so far worked uncompromisingly at creating a new monopolistic and monistic power structure. The negotiations between Demos' representatives and other political parties failed because Demos refused to make any concessions and insisted on having all the leading and decisive posts in its hands. Moreover, Demos' leaders made the acceptance of their programme a condition for participating in a possible coalition government. The result is that the three branches of power are, once again, in the hands of one political group.

In Parliament, Demos, first of all, curbed the independent political functioning of its constitutive parties. It suspended their particular political identities and claimed it directly represented the general, i.e. national interest. Its career in Parliament starts with disciplining its own MPs. Although its leaders advocated a secret ballot as long as they were in opposition, they suspended it when they gained power so that they could have 'their' MPs under control. They transformed them into a voting machine which could, by their numerical strength, outvote any proposal of the opposition without having to argue against it. This kind of 'party discipline', of course, outrules politics founded on public discussion. It also tends to transform Parliament into the executive of the Demos' leaders.

The second major achievement of Demos' leadership in the Parliament was to turn down the Liberals' proposal that MPs could be paid for their work by the state. The demagogic explanation of the new rulers was that they wanted to reduce the costs of the state apparatus.[25] In fact, they sapped the material basis of the oppositional parties whose electoral success should have enabled them to work normally.[26] This was an act directed against institutionalised political pluralism. On the other hand, Demos' leaders decided to employ their own MPs within the state apparatus, which they regard now as their property. In this way, they have turned the elected 'representatives of the people' into state employees. The idea seems to be to have agents of the legislature working in the executive power, while state secretaries are simultaneously appearing as parliamentarians and legislators. It is a telling detail that the Secretary for Defence became the spokesman of Demos' parliamentary club. What has been founded after the free elections is a new political patronage and its clientele.

The power of patrons is inevitably patriarchal power. In fact, women have almost disappeared from politics. The new mission designed for them is of course to give birth to as many new Slovenes as possible. The new democracy is male, phallocratic democracy. And if we understand women to be the biggest social minority, their new situation tells us what is happening, or is going to happen, to other minorities. They have become politically nonexistent, they are unrepresented and silenced. As society consists mainly of minorities, this is its prospect.

NSMs were badly defeated on elections and have submerged while public space has been invaded by new totalising ideologies of anti-communism and nationalism. This is where spontaneous totalitarianism from below meets with systematising totalitarian aspirations from above. In fact, since the new rulers have been in power, they have continually attempted to suppress the mass media and limit the liberty of the press. The growing influence of the politically revived catholicism is an important aspect of the process which could be described—to refer to the beginning of this chapter—as the cultural counter-revolution. It seems as if things have changed radically after a decade of liberty of a successful struggle against communism and for democracy. The new Minister of Culture has articulated the slogan for the 1990s: *Ora et labora!* Pray and work!

Notes

1. By 'this country' I mean Slovenia. NSM in Yugoslavia not only first appeared in Slovenia but remained its distinctive feature. Nothing comparable has happened in other Yugoslav republics, or regions. Consequently, this chapter deals with the Slovene case, and with Yugoslavia only as the context.
2. Forms of this repression are summarised in Mastnak 1989.
3. By this deprivation, society is dissolved into atomised individuals who are easier to master, while the compulsory aggregations make the surveillance over these social atoms more effective. Totalitarian deprivation of freedom of association is twofold.
4. See Lefort 1981, Lefort 1986.
5. 'Moral–political appropriateness' was a clause imposed in the 1970s to purge public offices of the persons who were not of the 'party line'. It is the Yugoslav counterpart of the *Berufsverbot* and was widely practised until recently, despite the fact that it blatantly violated the rights guaranteed by the Constitution. It is still practised in the Kosovo province to eliminate all those who are are not ready to be subjected unreservedly to the Serbian dictatorship.
6. The so-called Belgrade trial could be considered an important turning-point. A group of Slovene journalists brought the authors, whose reports from the trial prejudicated the guilt of the defendants, to the Court of Honour where they were found to have violated the professional codex. The verdicts of the Court of Honour were published and from that point on the coverage of the trial in the Slovene press improved. This was a great moral victory and of

importance for two main reasons. It proved that limits could be set to political dictate in the media as well as to political arbitrariness in the legal sphere.

7. Igor Vidmar, perhaps the most important organiser and 'ideologist' of the punk scene, was twice sentenced to a short-term imprisonment for wearing 'nazi' badges: the first was the famous Dead Kennedies' 'Nazi punks – f— off', and the other a CND badge.

8. A punk, when asked what punk means, replied: 'Punk was Solidarity in Poland at its beginnings.' Shortly after the imposition of martial law in Poland, a big rock concert in support of Solidarity was organised in Ljubljana (the money was sent to the victims of military repression); a smaller protest concert was held at the fist anniversary of Jaruzelski's dictatorship. Besides this, an anthology of the documents of the Polish opposition and writings of its leaders, 800 typescript pages, was published in Ljubljana in February 1982 (edited by Lev Kreft and myself). This happened at a time when our Belgrade colleagues were imprisoned for unfolding a Solidarity banner at a public meeting in Belgrade.

9. The first programmatic text which came from the West and initiated a discussion here was John Keane's letter to Paul Piccone on 'why civil society is important for socialists . . . and others' from 1983 (not published in English). In 1985 I edited a comprehensive anthology on the contemporary state–civil society discussion in East and West.

10. I discuss this more in detail in Mastnak 1989.

11. The term is used by a German journal (see *Alternative* 1982).

12. See Mastnak 1988. I use the term in opposition to the meaning given to it in Laclau Mouffe 1985, p. 188.

13. This case is discussed in Tomc 1989.

14. Now, at the time of the first free elections in Slovenia after the Second World War, the issue has reappeared.

15. Kant, *Der Streit der Fakultäten* (1794), Part II, §6 (see Kant, p. 358).

16. In 1986/7, opinion polls already reported that about 45 per cent of the Slovene population would participate in the NSMs while about 75 per cent were sympathetic to their ideas and actions.

17. I report on the congress in Mastnak 1987.

18. The Yugoslav Secretary of People's Defence visited Ethiopia to sell arms to a country in which millions were dying of hunger at the time. This was the only help the Yugoslav government offered to the friendly non-aligned country.

19. It finally fell apart early in 1990 as the Slovene delegation left the federal congress, and immediately after that renamed itself the Party of Democratic Reforms. It is only the Serbian communists and the JNA (assisted by the provinces of Vojvodina and Kosovo and the Republic of Montenegro whom the Serbian national-Bolsheviks had successfully subjected to their rule) who are still trying to rebuild it.

20. As I do not discuss the trial and the social resistance here, see Mastnak 1989a; see also Licht and Nikolic 1989.

21. I use the term in György Konrád's sense (see Konrád 1985).

22. See on this Lefort 1981 and Lefort 1986.

23. Now, a year later, it is clear that Serbia has in fact not only abolished the autonomy of the Kosovo province but established a regime there which can be described only as apartheid. The Albanians, who form nearly 90 per cent of the

local population, have been degraded to second-class citizens, deprived of political representation, removed from leading posts in industry and cultural institutions, their rights and liberties have been suspended, in schools and at work place segregation on national basis has been imposed, and state terrorism executed by the Serbian police and assisted by JNA, with dozens of people killed, massive arrests, political justice, poisoning of school children etc., is the way Serbian communists rule there.

24. Its neighbour in the South is the Republic of Croatia. Its being another sovereign nation-state has not prevented the Serbs living on its territory to arm themselves and harass those who are of another 'tribe'. The nationalist communist authorities in Belgrade support their 'brothers' in Croatia in their struggle against the Croat 'fascists' who are said to have attenuated the rights of the Serbian minority. They themselves have applied a policy of genocide in Kosovo. The new Slovene government believes this is happening in another state and is not particularly keen to meddle in 'foreign affairs'. This, however, does not demonstrate that Yugoslavia has fallen apart (which may in fact soon happen). For the time being it has returned to the state of nature.

25. I say 'demagogic' because Demos has not reduced the state apparatus, it has in fact enlarged it. It is worth mentioning that the political police has not been dissolved (as it had been promised and announced). Moreover, a new intelligence service is being formed with Parliament seemingly not having much say in the affair. Demos is also envisaging the formation of a Slovene army (the Greens, a member of the Demos coalition, have recently dissented from the idea and begun to opt—like the opposition—for a complete demilitarisation of Slovenia). Much more could be said on this account.

26. The old sources of financing were abolished, and living on membership fees is almost impossible when parties are only taking shape after half a century of suppression of political pluralism.

Bibliography (excluding Slovenian sources)

Alternative, 1982. Indiz 'Sprachlosigkeit', vol. 25, no.142.

Kant, I., 1986. *Werkausgabe*, vol. XI, Suhrkamp, Frankfurt/M.

Konrád, G., 1985. *Antipolitik, Mitteleuropäische Meditationen*, Suhrkamp, Frankfurt/M.

Laclau Mouffe, 1985. *Hegemony and Socialist Strategy*, Verso, London.

Lefort, C., 1981. *L'invention démocratique*, Fayard, Paris.

——1986. *Essais sur la politique XIXe-XXe siècles*, Seuil, Paris.

Licht, S., and Nikolić, M., 1989. 'Endless Crisis', *Across Frontiers*, vol. 4, no. 4 – Vol. 5, no. 1.

Mastnak, T., 1987. 'Even the future is not what it used to be', *Across Frontiers*, vol. 3, no. 3.

——1988. 'The implosion of the social: beyond radical democracy', in Mastnak, T., and Riha, R. (eds.), *The Subject in Democracy*, IMS ZRC SAZU, Ljubljana.

——1989. 'Modernization of repression', in V. Gathy (ed.), *State and Civil Society: Relationships in Flux*, Hungarian Academy of Sciences, Budapest.

——1989a. 'The night of the long knives', *Across Frontiers*, vol. 4, no. 4 – vol. 5, no. 1.

Melucci, A. (ed.), 1984. *Altri codici, Aree di movimento nello metropoli*, II Mulino, Bologna.
Melucci, A., 1985. 'The symbolic challenge of contemporary movements', *Social Research*, vol. 52, no. 4.
Tomc, G., 1989. 'Alternative politics. Example of the initiative for civil service', in V. Gathy (ed.), *State and Civil Society: Relationships in Flux*, Hungarian Academy of Sciences, Budapest.

Further reading

Arato, Andrew and Jean Cohen, forthcoming. *Civil Society and Democratic Theory*.
Jones, Lynne, 1990. *States of Change. A Central European diary: autumn 1989*, Merlin, London.
Keane, John, 1988. *Democracy and Civil Society*, Verso, London and New York.
Melucci, Alberto, 1989. *Nomads of the Present. Social movements and individual needs in contemporary society*, Hutchinson Radius, London.
Dalton, Russell and Manfred Keuchler (eds.), *Challenging the Political Order. New social and political movements in Western democracies*, Polity, Cambridge.

PART III
ECONOMIC GROWTH AND CHANGE

INTRODUCTION

James Simmie

In Part III we show how, despite the leading role of the Communist party, government and politics in determining the institutions and their goals in a socialist society, the underlying performance of its economy is still critical to its survival. Jože Mencinger and Bogomir Kovač show how economic problems have driven political reforms and how the limits of Marxist adaptations to inadequate economic performance have been reached. They also identify some of the technical difficulties involved in changing a socialist economy back into a market economy.

Both writers illustrate five main periods in the development of the socialist economy, ending with the fifth stage following the major economic reforms of the late 1980s. Jože Mencinger calls the previous four stages administrative socialism 1945 to 1952/3; administrative market socialism 1953 to 1962/3; market socialism 1963 to 1973/6; and contractual socialism 1974/6 to 1987/8.

According to Jože Mencinger two key elements of market economics were rejected when the system of contractual socialism was established. These were, first, markets as basic mechanisms for resource allocation, and second, macro-economic policy and indicative planning as a means of indirectly regulating economic activities. Instead, social contracts, self-management agreements and social planning were adopted.

This system was ideologically inspired, it sought to ignore the 'laws' of economics and was operated by too many institutions. The result was poor economic performance. Between 1960 and 1980 the Yugoslav economy grew by only 70 per cent of the corresponding increases in Southern European market economies. Growth stagnated in the 1980s. Even 'official' unemployment rose to 16 per cent. Hyperinflation had set in by 1989.

This poor economic performance, as much as anything else, led to the reform programme launched in 1988. Its objectives were no less than to create new, integral product, labour and capital markets. As Jože Mencinger points out, these are incompatible with social property and self-management. The stage has been set for a full-scale return to capitalism.

One prerequisite of a capitalist system is private property ownership in some form. In 1989 four types of ownership were established: social, co-operative, mixed and unlimited domestic, and foreign private ownership. This marked the transition from self-management to capitalist relationships in the economy. Of themselves, however, such changes leave many problems unresolved. Among them are continuing unemployment and regional problems.

Bogomir Kovač examines one of the major problems involved in changing from a collective to a market economy. This is the complex technical problem of turning a Basic Organisation of Associated Labour into a capitalist, market organisation. In the contractual socialist system business decisions were made by a triumvirate of workers' councils, managers and the state. Business policy was therefore quite different from that of market firms. Losses were covered by the banks! Accounting and budgetary procedures were extremely 'soft'.

Proposals for reform have included tighter financial controls and entrepreneurial development. Both pose major technical difficulties. In the first place, as Bogomir Kovač points out, it is very difficult to put a realistic value or price on a firm without the operation of an existing capital market. This means that Western accountants would find it extremely awkward to decide how much capital a firm was employing and therefore whether it was making a profit or not.

In the second place, it is hard to privatise a firm without some idea of what it is worth. Four different strategies have been adopted in Yugoslavia to overcome this problem. One technique has been to establish holding companies. The resources of Basic Organisations of Associated Labour are put into such companies and one of their main tasks is to convert their finances to a 'normal' accounting basis.

Another technique has been to distribute shares to workers on the basis of their past contributions to the Association. This is complex and does not necessarily mean that they can then be sold to other buyers. A third device involves selling shares to managers and workers. This also hits the problem of how to arrive at an initial price for those shares. Finally, some sales have been made to newly formed 'democratic' financial institutions. These include pension funds and the emerging insurance sector.

All these emerging techniques lead Bogomir Kovač to argue that social ownership is a socialist relic. He and Jože Mencinger both show how collective, socialist solutions to running the Yugoslav economy and its individual enterprises/associations have foundered upon poor economic performance. In this sense the ideological freedom of manoeuvre of the Communist party seems to have been limited by 'inevitable' economic forces. This paradoxically both reinforces and denies the basic Marxist assertion of the importance of the economy in determining other aspects of the political economy. It demonstrates the importance of the economy in circumscribing the realms of what is possible. At the same time it also shows that collective economies are not the inevitable direction of change, primarily because they have failed to solve the problem of economic growth and have not compensated their workers for this failure with greater *equality* in the distribution of wealth and resources.

5 FROM A CAPITALIST TO A CAPITALIST ECONOMY?

Jože Mencinger

Systemic changes, 1945–1988

In the theory of economic systems, the Yugoslav economy serves as the only example of what is called the self-managed, the participatory, the labour-managed or the socialist market economy. Benjamin Ward's 'Illyrian firm', Evsey Domar's 'producers' co-operative', Jaroslav Vanek's 'labour-managed market economy', and Branko Horvat's 'realistic model' have all been directly or indirectly inspired by the particularities of the Yugoslav institutional setting. This setting, however, has not been particularly stable and has often differed considerably from its theoretical blueprints. Since 1945 four distinct systemic types can be distinguished:

— administrative socialism (1945–52);
— administrative market socialism (1953–62);
— market socialism (1963–73); and
— contractual socialism (1974–88), followed by the collapse of socialism.

The starting years of the periods are the same as those in which new constitutions were passed. Such periodisation can be subject to criticism. First, it creates the notion that abrupt changes occurred in those years, which they did not. Second, some far-reaching institutional changes preceded constitutional changes; some followed them in consecutive years. Third, the gaps between the ideology embodied in constitutions, the actual normative setting and the reality have always been wide. Fourth, some economic policy changes have had much greater impact on actual economic development than systemic changes. The 1965 economic reform, which was dominated by macro-economic policy change (Bajt 1984, Burkett 1983), has even been considered the turning-point between the 'more successful' and the 'less successful' period of labour management (Horvat 1971, Sapir 1980). The same is true with respect to 1980, when the change of economic policy forced by the country's indebtedness caused a similar turning-point in all measurable performance indicators. The periodisation is, however, closely related to changes in the formal allocation of decision-making in the economy.

Adminstrative socialism, 1945-52

The major goal of adminstrative socialism was to tranform the underdeveloped, predominantly agricultural, capitalist society into an industrial socialist society. The means employed to bring about the transformation can only in part be attributed to the faith of the new political élite in the supremacy of the new system over a market economy; they were also in part intended to eliminate political competition and social pluralism. The organisation of the economy was modelled after the Soviet pattern; all basic economic problems such as valuation, organisation of production, income distribution, savings and investments were to be solved by centrally planned solutions. Enterprises were agents of the planners obliged to fulfil their instructions.

Rigidly planned economy was at the time believed to be the only viable socialist economy and the transformation into it was to be achieved by nationalising most of the means of production. The principle of control over the private sector was included in the Constitution of 1946, by stipulating that private property could be expropriated if so required by very extendable 'common interest'. Soon, nearly all non-agricultural economic activity was socialised. In the agricultural sector the anti-peasant policy was brought forward by compulsory deliveries and forced collectivisation.

Administrative market socialism, 1953-62

After 1952, Yugoslavia started to move from centralised economic planning, by reducing administrative constraints and making the enterprises more independent. The official birth of the new system can be traced to the Law on Management of Government Business Enterprises and Higher Economic Associations by Workers' Collectives, enacted in 1950, which proclaimed self-management as its foundation. However, its basic legal and political features were explicitly defined in the Constitution Act of 1953. These features were clearly summarised by Bičanić (Bičanić, 1957). He enumerated the differences between the new and the old system as follows:

1. social ownership of the means of production as opposed to the state ownership;

2. reliance on the market mechanism for the allocation of goods and services as opposed to the administrative mechanism;
3. increased use of financial instruments as opposed to adoption of simple administrative rules;
4. free distribution of available income by workers' councils as opposed to administratively fixed wages;
5. decentralised and functional budgeting at all administrative levels as opposed to an all-embracing state budget;
6. the rehabilitation of consumer sovereignty as opposed to the treatment of personal consumption as residual; and
7. the acceptance of independent farmers as opposed to compulsory collectivisation.

The reasons for the first and by far the most radical reform have not yet been fully explained. According to 'official beliefs', shared by some Western scholars, the reform was contemplated by the Yugoslav political leaders long before the break with the Soviet Union. The opinion that the workers' self-management was 'in the air before it was officially introduced by the government' (Gurvitch 1966) can, however, hardly be proved by actual developments before or after the break. On the contrary, the organisation of the economy, the overwhelming nationalisation of practically every economic activity including typical non-capitalist forms of production, and the increased pressure for forced collectivisation in agriculture after the break with the Soviet Union, indicate the opposite. Furthermore, the Yugoslav political leaders were, until the time of the break, fully engaged in recasting the Yugoslav economy into a Soviet-type planned economy. To Boris Kidrič, the person who dominated economic thought and who was one of the architects of the administrative system, state ownership was, up to 1950, 'the highest form of the ownership of the means of production, and planning was the fundamental law of socialist development' (Kidrič 1949a, 1950a). In less than one year, the standing of state ownership was altered to being 'only the first and the shortest step of the socialist revolution; the building of socialism requires the transformation of state socialism into a free association of direct producers' (Kidrič 1950b). The ability of both Yugoslav politicians and its social scientists to reread and reinterpret Marx according to daily needs was established for the first time (but not the last). Thus, while bad economic results and the need to adapt to the new environment were certainly important, the ideological and political rather than economic issues were decisive in searching for new, non-Soviet, forms of socialism. The opinon that something had to be invented quickly to give the break a symbol rather than, at least at first, to engage in a full-fledged systemic reform (Rusinow 1977) appears to be close to the truth.

In reality, self-management was rather limited, even in the normative setting, and much more so in practice. In principle workers took over the entrepreneurial function, but in reality both the distribution of enterprise income and the investment decisions remained centralised. The development strategy remained essentially Soviet, the political system and the policy of no social pluralism remained firm.

Market socialism, 1963–73

The entire systemic development during the 1950s and 1960s was a process of permanent reforms. All imaginable solutions were tried, often in a very uncoordinated manner (Čičin-Šain 1985). Numerous and very varied economic instruments were being used and each new economic instrument tended to change the given structure and the system as such. Nevertheless, throughout this period, the economy was gradually and essentially becoming market-based, although neither the labour nor the capital market were officially sanctioned, and both have remained underdeveloped.

Among permanent changes, two reforms, in 1961 and in 1965, should be noted as those which decisively reduced central control and increased the autonomy of economic units considerably. In the 1961 reform, wage control was abolished, foreign trade was liberalised, the economy, which up to that time was virtually closed, was made susceptible to the influences of the world market, and the monetary and banking systems were radically overhauled. However, 'the three reforms of 1961 were poorly prepared, partly inconsistent and badly implemented' (Horvat 1971, p. 83), and even more elaborate systemic changes (with macro-economic policy changes they were to be designated as the Economic Reform of 1965) took place in the years 1964–7. The changes affected investment mechanisms, the foreign trade system, the monetary and banking systems, the tax system and the price system. The general investment funds of governments at all levels were abolished and their assets and liabilities transferred to banks. The banking system was restructured and the banks could now be established and managed by groups of enterprises. The National Bank was transformed into a monetary institution. The reform of the investment system included tax cuts which, it was hoped, would enable enterprises to finance more of their investments. The turnover tax which had been levied at various rates in different sectors was replaced by the retail sales tax. The prices were restructured so as to resemble more closely the world prices. The liberalisation of foreign trade was widened by reducing tariff rates and abolishing licensing.

Market liberalisation combined with restrictive macro-economic policy produced predictable, though not anticipated, results. The growth of the economy slowed down. Social and political consequences of rapidly increasing unemployment could be alleviated only by a massive exodus of workers. The cost-push inflationary pressures emerged from the combination of increased freedom of enterprises in income distribution and the increased 'softness' of their budget constraint, resulting in high inflation. The balance of trade worsened and the Yugoslav share in the world exports started to decline. In short, the aspirations of the reformers were not realised, and the economic reform has been more and more considered a failure, marking the end of the 'Yugoslav economic miracle' (Sapir 1980).

Poor economic performance was accompanied by the even less desirable development in the social and political domains. Social property, defined as property of 'each and all', degenerated into group property (Bajt 1980). The inequalities among individuals and among regions increased, causing social and political tensions among republics. Furthermore, the concentration of economic power in the hands of managerial élite-technocrats (though predominantly members of the party) threatened to deprive the party bureaucracy of political control. This threat, it appears, was the most important reason for the counter-reforms.

Contractual socialism, 1974–88

The solution was found in inventing a new version of a socialist economy, one which would preserve its 'basic orientations' permanently. The new economic model was shaped by Edvard Kardelj, the politician-ideologue who dominated economic and political thought in Yugoslavia for more than twenty years. The system was legalised by the Constitution of 1974 and the Associated Labour Act of 1976. In subsequent years parts of the system were gradually adapted to conform with these laws. The whole system was affected, and an entirely new and rather awkward terminology was invented. The Basic Organisation of Associated Labour (BOAL) became the basic economic unit. The official proclamation that maximisation of income is the basic objective of BOALs, as well as Working Organisations (WOs, or enterprises) and Composed Organisations of Associated Labour (COALs) 'resolved' the old debate on the objective of a self-managed firm, which started when Ward's 'natural and rational' objective (Ward 1958), although accepted by most foreign economists (Domar 1966, Vanek 1970, Sapir, 1980) was criticised in Yugoslavia (Horvat 1972, Dubravčić 1970).

Although formally the basic elements of the socialist market system were to be retained, the changes were so far-reaching that the market character of the Yugoslav economy was put into question. The associated labour concept, to a considerable extent, rejected two key components of the market economy: market as the basic mechanism for resource allocation, and macro-economic policy and indicative planning as a means of indirect regulation of economic activities. It insisted that these were to be substituted to the greatest extent possible by mechanisms of social contracts, self-management agreements and social planning.

The system had at least three important deficiencies. First, it was based on ideologically inspired self-serving perceptions of the reality, which led to unrealistic performance expectations. Second, the principles of economic theory were simply overlooked or ignored. Third, the system was overloaded with institutions. The inoperative blueprints and/or the undesirable results of the system required government interventions. Suspended or irrelevant 'rules of the game' had to be replaced daily by an enormous amount of administrative measures and incessant changes in legislation. The system as a consequence gradually acquired many characteristics of administrative systems, such as rigidness, slowness, inconsistency of administrative measures, distrust of economic units by administrators, and the application of non-economic means for the implementation of economic goals.

Economic performance

The vast majority of studies analysing the performance of the socialist self-managed economy has been directed to micro-economic issues. The performance has been judged predominantly by deductive analysis, comparing the behaviour of the worker-managed firm to that of the capitalist firm under different assumptions concerning objective functions, production functions, institutional constraints on labour and capital supply, and environmental conditions. Macro-economics of the labour-managed economy has been much less analysed, though both theoretical and empirical studies of macro-economic performance exist (Tyson 1980, Estrin and Bartlett 1983, Burkett 1983, Bajt 1986).

The two most prominent scholars in the field of labour-managed economy, Vanek and Horvat, have stressed its macro-economic advantages. Vanek's (1970) conclusions about the expected performance of the self-managed economy are extremely favourable. Horvat (1972) arrived at similarly favourable macro-economic implications. According to him, high rates of growth are assured by a higher propensity to invest due to reduced risk and uncertainty, full employment by the reluctance of workers to dismiss fellow workers, and price stability by the absence of the fundamental employee–employer conflict.

The above three macro-economic propositions by Vanek and Horvat were tested against the Yugoslav reality in the 1971–7 period (Mencinger 1979). Only the proposition of stability in employment and growth rates was confirmed, but the promotion of growth and long-term price stability were not. On the other hand, evidence of the strong economic performance of the Yugoslav economy was provided by early empirical studies (Balassa and Bertrand 1970). The performance has often been described as impressive before 1965, and the declines after 1965 were attributed to changes in external conditions and in relative weights given to various economic objectives, and only partly to the system which weakened macro-economic policy-making (World Bank 1979).

Major macro-economic performance indicators show that performance in the period of administrative socialism (1947–52) was bad, in the period of administrative market socialism (1953–62) rather good, in the period of market socialism (1963–73) fair, and in the period of contractual socialism (1974–88) meagre. Simultaneous movements over time of the capital/output and labour/output ratios indicate that the dynamic efficiency of the economy is related to systemic changes (Mencinger, 1986). In the period of administrative socialism (1945–52), economic growth was achieved by enormous increases in inputs, both ratios increasing rapidly. When rigid planning was abolished and the sovereignty of planners was replaced by that of consumers and independent producers (1953–62), our two ratios decreased rapidly. In the third period (1963–73), the capital/output ratio started to grow again, while the labour/output ratio decreased only slowly. The changes which made relatively abundant labour expensive, as the majority of taxes and contributions were levied on wages, and scarce capital a virtually free good, with real interest rates negative, appear to be the important causes of the deterioration. The situation worsened further in the period of 'contractual socialism' (since 1973), when the capital/output ratio started to increase rapidly and the labour/output ratio first stagnated and then, after 1980, began to increase.

The growth rates in Table 5.1 appear satisfactory when compared with those of developed market economies. Comparison with countries at a level of development similar to that of Yugoslavia, however, suggests that this growth performance was fairly typical, except for the excellent agricultural results in the period 1953–62, following the abandonment of the policy of forced collectivisation. A faster growth of industrial production in the second period, compared to the first, is also in evidence, although this is partly the fruit of huge investments in the first period in projects with long lead times. Furthermore, the shares of investment in GNP suggest that the cost of growth in Yugoslavia was high and, indirectly, that despite reforms, the country retained the Soviet pattern of development. The increase of GNP per unit of investment in the 1960–80 period was only 70 per cent of the corresponding increase in comparable market economies of Southern Europe (Bajt 1987).

In the 1950s and 1960s Yugoslavia succeeded, despite the difficulties, irrationalities and waste which characterised post-war development, in maintaining relatively high growth rates, price stability, rising standards of living and reasonable indebtedness. Relative success came to an end in the 1970s when the Yugoslav economic system started to demonstrate its weaknesses and Yugoslav society started to disintegrate. Due to remittances and injections of foreign loans, this was not visible and the crisis was postponed. It started with the 'foreign debts' crisis'.

Table 5.1 The main performance indicators of the Yugoslav economy, 1946–88

Period	1946–52[1]	1952–62	1963–73	1974–88	1980–88
(average annual rates of growth, in per cent)					
GNP	2.3	8.2	6.5	3.3	0.6
Industry	12.9	12.2	8.6	5.0	2.4
Agriculture	−3.1	9.2	3.1	2.1	0.0
Employment	8.3	6.8	2.4	3.4	2.2
Exports in US$	−3.1	12.0	14.0	11.3	8.0
Imports in US$	3.6	10.1	16.6	11.3	−0.8
Investments		11.5	5.3	0.7	−8.0
Consumption		6.5	6.4	2.2	−1.0
Prices		3.6	13.0	42.3	80.2
(ratios, in per cent, except rows 3 and 4)					
Unemployment rate		5.01	7.58	13.29	14.24
Export/import rate		64.44	69.44	67.96	87.81
Labour/output ratio[2]		3.87	2.42	1.87	1.90
Capital/output ratio		2.28	2.23	2.68	2.97
Investment/GDP rate		41.99	38.87	35.21	28.60

Source: Statistical Yearbook, different years.

Notes:
1. Horvat, 1971.
2. 1974–84 instead of 1974–86, and 1980–4 instead of 1980–6.

Economic performance in the last period is therefore characterised by the break in 1980, dividing the more and the less successful subperiods (see Table 5.2). This is superficial. Namely, in the 1970s, excess demand was reduced on account of the persistent balance of payments deficit. The availability and low costs of foreign credits also favoured accumulation of debt. The share of foreign supply (imports–exports) in gross available product was for several years in the range of 5 to 10 per cent (depending on the exchange rate used in calculations). As a result, performance indicators reflecting 'internal balance' are satisfactory before 1980, while developments in the 'external balance' are unfavourable. The 1980s differ considerably: deterioration in internal balance is accompanied by improvements in external balance. The success before 1980 was thus fictitious; yearly inflows of foreign capital were greater than increases of the gross domestic product. The Yugoslav economy was doomed to stagnate for a decade if there were no net foreign capital inflows. When the possibility of development based on foreign accumulation faded and when the accumulated debts required an enormous outflow of capital for debt servicing, the fictitious success dissolved as well.

The 'price' for achieving external equilibrium was high. It consisted of stagnation coupled with decreased efficiency (represented by the increases in the capital/output and labour/output ratios), unemployment, inflation and increased interregional disparities. The annual growth of GNP decreased from 6.1 per cent in the period 1971–9 to stagnation in the 1980s. The unemployment rate reached 16 per cent at the end of 1988. The average inflation rate increased from 20 per cent in the 1971–9 period to 40 per cent between 1980 and 1984, to 140 per cent in 1987, and finally turned to hyperinflation in 1989. Real wages lowered to two-thirds of their level in 1979 and interregional differences increased. While acceleration of inflation was initiated by the squeeze of domestic supplies, other factors contributed as well. Cuts in imports reduced competition and the devaluations of the dinar increased production costs, which were readily passed on to domestic prices. After 1983, inflationary expectations set in, and they soon became the single most important factor transforming high inflation into hyperinflation.

Table 5.2 Performance of the Yugoslav economy in the 1980s

| | internal balance | | | external balance | efficiency | |
	(1)	(2)	(3)	(4)	(5)	(6)
1953–63	8.2	3.6	5.0	64.7	2.28	3.87
1963–73	6.5	13.0	7.6	69.4	2.23	2.42
1974–80	5.7	20.1	13.3	55.6	2.64	1.86
1981	1.5	44.8	13.5	70.2	2.69	1.79
1982	0.5	31.0	14.1	77.8	2.82	1.84
1983	−1.0	38.1	14.6	81.6	2.96	1.89
1984	2.0	56.3	15.3	84.5	2.95	1.89
1985	0.5	75.4	16.0	87.2	2.97	1.91
1986	3.5	88.1	16.2	84.1	2.95	1.91
1987	−1.0	118.4	15.7	91.3	3.01	1.97
1988	−2.0	198.8	16.4	96.5	3.13	2.01

Source: Statistical Yearbook, different years.

(1) GNP growth; (2) inflation rate; (3) unemployment rate; (4) export/import ratio; (5) capital/output ratio; (6) labour/output ratio.

The breakdown

The collapse of the socialist economic system in Yugoslavia in general, and of the so-called contractual socialism, in particular, has become obvious in the 1980s, not only because of poor economic performance but also on purely speculative grounds. The system was based on ideologically inspired perceptions of reality, it overlooked the principles of economic theory, and was overloaded with institutions. Before 1980, the problems which should have been dealt with were instead 'resolved' by irrelevant ideological statements. The criticism of contractual socialism on efficiency grounds was vigorously refuted as hostile to self-management and socialism. However, when in the 1980s the economic situation developed into a profound economic, social, political and moral crisis, a variety of ideas concerning the right way out of the overwhelming crisis appeared and was particularly wide in academic debates. A number of solutions were suggested, and in the process most of the taboo topics were opened (Horvat 1985, Jerovšek et al. 1985). These include, to name a few, recognition of labour and capital markets as indispensable segments of the market economy, calls for changes in the principles of self-management (Goldstein 1985), the questioning of the concept of social property and the suggestion to replace it by collective property (Bajt 1986), and the restoration of a truly mixed economy (Popović 1984).

Official attempts at a new reform started in 1982, with the 'Long-Term Stabilisation Programme' (Savezni društveni savet, 1984). Most Yugoslav economists participated. The result was a highly eclectic and inconsistent programme, drawing ideas from all schools of economic thought, from extreme monetarism to orthodox Keynesian, often nicely cloaked in Marxian terminology. Its main orientation was nevertheless clear: the reintroduction of the market and a reduced role of 'contractual' institutions. However, it was 'too late and too little'.

While economic reforms in the past enabled Yugoslavia to adapt to global structural changes more rapidly than the other socialist countries, mere economic reform could not help any more. First, new changes of the economic system which would remain within the Marxian ideology were no longer feasible. The situation required the abandonment of ideology. Second, the proven ability of Yugoslavia to change systems, revaluate Marxism and redefine socialism and to push the trade-off between ideology and pragmatism in favour of the latter was no longer there. Yugoslavia had reached the point where any economic reforms unaccompanied by political reforms could only increase the inconsistency between the economic system and the political system.

While party ideologists and economists speculated about other types of socialism, the federal government in 1988 created a new Commission

(Mikulić's Commission), which quickly launched a new 'Programme of Economic Reform'. Contrary to expectations and scepticism, its reform proposals were, although theoretically confused and inconsistent, ideologically extremely radical.

The programme launched in 1988 required the creation of an 'integral market' consisting of product, labour and capital markets, which had existed in a rudimentary form but which had not been accepted on the ideological and theoretical level. 'Official' introduction of markets for factors of production, however, required the recognition of the consequences, which were devastating for the premises of the existing economic system; in short, social property and self-management cannot coexist with the capital and labour market. The new systemic laws based on the reform proposals thus set the stage for nothing else but a wholesale return to capitalism. The unique institutional framework of the Yugoslav economy (social ownership and self-management distinguishing it from the market economies, absence of any meaningful planning, and stronger reliance on markets distinguishing it from centrally planned economies) had apparently come to its end.

The constitutional conditions for the reform were created by a set of Amendments to the Constitution, adopted in November 1988. The document containing a general outline of the current reform, 'The Principles of the Economic System Reform', adopted in October 1988, and systemic laws regulating economy and labour relations, adopted in 1988 and 1989, were much more radical. The most important among them, the Enterprise Act, passed in late December 1988, in fact altered the Yugoslav economic system. It re-established enterprise (succeeding previous work organisations, BOALs, etc.) as a legal entity engaged in economic activities and fully responsible for its business operations. Four types of ownership: social, co-operative, mixed, and unlimited domestic and foreign private ownership of the means of production were introduced. The 'self-management relationships' were in fact replaced with 'capital relationships'; socialism was replaced with capitalism.

One of the basic ideological and practical problems faced by the reform has been to reassign decision-making authority and managing rights, which were previously, at least on the ideological level, exclusively given to labour. By acknowledging private ownership of the means of production, the monopoly of the workers over decision-making has become self-contradictory. On the other hand, such a control of management by the owners of capital is self-contradictory to workers' self-management. A compromise was found by retaining reduced decision-making by workers within social enterprises and recognising a kind of co-management of workers within mixed and private enterprises.

Economic reform is well under way. Most ideological questions have been resolved or ignored. Paradoxically, the present economic and social crises which prompted changes are, at the same time, the major obstacle to changes. Unemployment and enormous regional differences are the two most important among them.

The implications of unemployment figures in Yugoslavia differ from the implications of comparative figures for a developed industrial country in many respects. The characteristics of labour supply and demand make Yugoslav unemployment basically a long-term and regional problem. Labour supply is determined by the developing nature of the country with relatively high birth rates, a high percentage of agricultural population and specific ownership structure, predominant socialist non-agricultural and predominant private agricultural sectors. Rapid industrialisation, the spread of technological progress in agriculture, differences in real wages, and economic policy inspired by ideological prejudices, caused a quick one-way flow of labour from the agricultural to the non-agricultural sector. Agriculture became the most important source of labour for the non-agricultural sector, and a buffer against the social and political effects of unemployment. The demand for labour was determined by the long-term scarcity of capital, which implies a complementary rather than substitutional relation between labour and capital. This was amplified by underpriced capital, which favoured capital intensive projects, and ideological constraints, which induced the transfer of private capital (especially from workers abroad) into consumption and non-productive investments (cars, housing) instead of productive investments.

Table 5.3 Employment and unemployment in thousands, in per cent

Year	(1)	(2)	(3)	(4)	(5)	(6)	(7)	(8)
1960	159	5.48	2,903	2,821	81	2.81	240	8.29
1965	236	6.61	3,582	3,356	226	6.31	463	12.92
1970	319	8.48	3,764	3,530	233	6.21	553	14.70
1975	540	11.57	4,666	4,038	628	13.46	1,167	25.04
1980	785	13.82	5,680	5,107	573	10.09	1,358	23.91
1985	1,039	16.30	6,377	5,318	1,068	16.63	2,100	32.93
1986	1,086	16.55	6,565	5,465	1,100	16.76	2,187	33.31
1987	1,080	16.12	6,703	5,404	1,298	19.36	2,378	35.48
1988	1,128	16.78	6,719	5,320	1,399	20.82	2,527	37.61

(1) number of registered job seekers; (2) registered unemployment rate; (3) number of workers (socialised sector); (4) 'required' number of workers; (5) number of workers; (6) disguised unemployment rate; (7) total unemployment; (8) total unemployment rate.

The changed structure of unemployment (young people concentrated in industrial centres rather than unskilled workers dispersed in villages) will affect the social and political dimensions of the problem. In addition, at least 20 per cent of those employed in the socialist sector should be considered superfluous, and a total of about 1.4 million workers should be added to registered job seekers when estimating the unemployed labour resources (see Table 5.3). Regional disparities also appear to be one of the major obstacles to future economic development, and even more so for changes in the economic and political systems. They have actually increased despite efforts to equalise development levels throughout the country (see Table 5.4). Three regions (Slovenia, Croatia and Vojvodina) stand above the Yugoslav average, while the position of Serbia proper is somewhat vague. Slovenia clearly stands out at one end and Kosovo somewhat less conspicuously at the other end of the development scale. The GNP per capita between them widened from 5:1 in 1955, to 7:1 in 1987. In

Table 5.4 Regional developments of Yugoslavia

	YU	BIH	CG	H	M	SL	SR	1	2	3
					rates					
(1)	0.277	0.277	0.248	0.327	0.245	0.423	0.252	0.276	0.120	0.295
(2)	0.417	0.365	0.405	0.527	0.411	0.690	0.405	0.427	0.232	0.460
(3)	0.153	0.228	0.232	0.075	0.262	0.018	0.193	0.169	0.491	0.154
			indexes (Yugoslavia = 100)							
(4)	100	69	77	125	65	197	91	99	28	120
(5)	100	83	77	122	68	175	86	91	43	94
(6)	100	88	88	100	82	126	99	98	70	110
(7)	100	87	87	102	100	129	89	85	106	95
			growth rates 1956–83							
(8)	5.7	5.3	5.9	5.3	5.9	6.0	6.0	5.9	5.7	6.2
(9)	0.9	1.2	1.1	0.5	1.4	0.8	1.0	0.8	2.4	0.5
			ratios							
(10)	2.85	3.44	4.35	2.85	2.85	2.70	2.56	2.44	4.00	2.83
(11)	6.36	7.09	9.52	6.80	6.99	5.62	5.92	5.46	11.00	5.98

YU–Yugoslavia; BIH–Bosnia and Hercegovina; CG–Montenegro; H–Croatia; M–Macedonia; SL–Slovenia; SR–Serbia; 1–Serbia proper; 2–Kosovo; 3–Vojvodina. (1) participation rate (1984); (2) net participation rate (1984); (3) unemployment rate (1984); (4) GSP/capita(1983) (Yugoslavia = 100); (5) GSP/capita (1955); (6) GSP/employee (1983), (7) GSP/employee (1955); (8) GSP growth; (9) population growth; (10) capital/output ratio (1983); (11) marginal capital/output ratio, 1971–83.

addition, the intraregional differences are considerable throughout Yugoslavia.

There are four main factors affecting interregional disparities, with very limited prospects of reducing them: demographic movements, differences in productivity between modern non-agricultural and backward agricultural sectors, differences in productivity within sectors, and low mobility of labour from the south to the north. Any sizeable reduction of regional disparities will therefore be slow and expensive. Reduction of disparities might be accompanied by increased political tensions aggravated by increased nationalism.

The outcome of the reforms remains blurred for many reasons, although economic collapse appears inevitable also for many reasons. First, the ideological and political reforms, if this term can be used for sweeping transformations, went much further than envisaged, and the ideological disintegration and political metamorphosis have been too radical and too fast to be accompanied by the needed structural adjustments. Second, the technological gap between Yugoslavia and market economies has widened, and Yugoslavia is unable to accommodate rapidly to world production standards. Third, decades of Marxism and collectivism have adversely influenced working patterns and value judgements. Finally, unstable equilibrium within the country, based on the belief in unconflicting interests, has apparently come to its end, and the break of the 'unified' Yugoslav economy appears very likely. Three outcomes, although not equally likely, appear to be possible: (1) further centralisation of the economic system; (2) a confederation; or (3) a complete political disintegration of Yugoslavia.

Consequently, the transition from the pre-reform socialist economy to the post-reform market economy, which would, even under the most favourable conditions, represent a considerable challenge, will prove to be a painful process. It will be accompanied by economic, social and political tensions emerging from redistribution of income, wealth and power between individuals, social strata, nations and republics. Expected outcomes of the transition from a socialist to a market economy are in most cases based on a lack of realism. Illusions that the reforms will transform Yugoslavia instantly into a welfare state have been created. The disappointing outcomes in the early stages of transition could therefore pull the process back towards traditional socialist arrangements or could incite complete political disintegration of the country.

References

Bajt, A., 1980. 'La propriété sociale en tant que propriété de tous et de chacun', in *Revue d'études comparatives est–ouest*, 11, 41–72.

———1984. 'Trideset godina privrednog rasta', *Ekonomist*, 38, 1–20 (German translation in *Socialistische Theorie und Praxis*, 13 (1986) 34–62.

———1986. 'Preduzetništvo u samoupravnoj socijalističkoj privredi' *Privredna kretanja*, 159, 32–46.

———1987. 'Stvarni i potencijalni društveni proizvod 1980', *Privredna kretanja*, 171, 42–52.

———1988. *Samoupravna oblika družbene lastnine*, Globus, Zagreb.

Balassa, B. and Bertrand, J., 1970. 'Growth performance of Eastern European countries', *American Economic Review* (proceedings), 60, 314–20.

Bićanić, R., 1957. 'Economic growth under centralised and decentralised planning: Yugoslavia—a case study', *Economic Development and Cultural Change*, vol. 5, 63–74.

Burkett, J., 1983. *The Effects of Economic Reform in Yugoslavia: investment and trade policy, 1959-1976*, IIS, University of California.

Ćićin-Šain, A., 1985. 'The development and role of the major economic policy instruments in Yugoslavia 1952-1972', in Gey et al., *Sozialismus und Industrialisierung*, Campus Verlag, Frankfurt, pp. 175–96.

Domar, E.D., 1966: 'The Soviet collective farm', *American Economic Review*, vol. 56, 734–57.

Dubravčić, D., 1970. 'Labour as entrepreneurial input: an essay in the theory of the producers' cooperative economy', *Economica*, 297–310.

Estrin, S. and Bartlett, W., 1983. 'The effects of enterprise self-management in Yugoslavia: an empirical survey', in Jones, D.C. (ed.), *Participatory and self-managed firms*, Lexington Books, Lexington, Mass., 83–109.

Goldstein, S., 1985 *Prijedlog 85*, Scientia Yugoslavica, Zagreb.

Gurvitch, G., 1966. 'Les conseils ouvriers', *Autogestion*, no. 1, 50–7.

Horvat, B., 1971. 'Yugoslav economic policy in the post-war period: problems, ideas, institutional developments', *American Economic Review* (supplement), vol. 61, no. 2, 71–169.

———1972. 'Critical notes on the theory of the labour-managed firm and some macroeconomic implications', *Economic Analysis*, vol. 6, 291–4.

———1985. *Jugoslovensko društvo u krizi*, Globus, Zagreb.

Jerovšek, J. et al., 1985. *Kriza, blokade i perspektive*, Globus, Zagreb.

Kidrič, B., 1949a. 'Kvalitet robnonovčanih odnosa u FNRJ', *Komunist* 1/49, 33–51.

———1950a. *Privredni problemi FNRJ*, Belgrade.

———1950b. 'Teze o ekonomici prelaznog razdoblja u našoj zemlji', *Komunist* 6/ 1950, 1–20.

Mencinger, J., 1979. 'Theoretical and actual performance of the worker-managed economy', *Economic Analysis*, vol. 13, 253–65.

———1986. 'The Yugoslav economic systems and their efficiency', *Economic Analysis*, vol. 19, 31–43.

Popović, S., 1984. *Ogled o jugoslovenskom privrednom sistemu*, Marksistički centar Beograd.

Rusinow, D., 1977. *The Yugoslav experiment 1948-1974*, University of California, Berkeley.

Sapir, A., 1980. 'Economic growth and factor substitution: what happened to the Yugoslav economic miracle?', *Economic Journal*, vol. 90, 294–313.

Tyson, L., 1980. *The Yugoslav economic system and its performance in the 1970s*, University of California, Berkeley.

Vanek, J., 1970. *The general theory of labour-managed economies*, Cornell University Press, Ithaca.

——1972. 'The macroeconomic theory and policy of an open worker managed economy', *Economic Analysis*, vol. 6, 255–69.

Ward, B., 1958. 'The firm in Illyria: market syndicalism', *American Economic Review*, vol. 48, 566–89.

——1984. *Dugoročni program ekonomske stabilizacije*, Belgrade.

Savezno izvršno veće, 1988. *Osnove reforme privrednog sistema*, Belgrade.

World Bank, 1979. *Yugoslavia: selfmanagement socialism and the challenges of development*, Johns Hopkins University Press, Baltimore.

Further reading

Burkett, J., 1983. *Economic reform in Yugoslavia*, University of California, Berkeley.

UN ECE, 1988. *Economic reforms in the European centrally planned economies*, New York.

Vanek, J., 1970. *The general theory of labour-managed economies*, Cornell University Press, Ithaca.

World Bank, 1979. *Yugoslavia: selfmanagement socialism and the challenges of development*, Johns Hopkins University Press, Baltimore.

6 ENTREPRENEURSHIP AND PRIVATISATION OF SOCIAL OWNERSHIP IN ECONOMIC REFORMS

Bogomir Kovač

Introduction

The Yugoslav social crises of the 1980s are, like the crises in other European socialist countries, proof of the political, ideological and economic breakdown of socialism. It means that its fundamental institutions need to be abolished or fundamental reform has to be carried out. No doubt socialism is the most influential social ideology of the twentieth century. At the very beginning it offered itself as a complete political and economic system (social ownership, planning, income distribution according to work performed, indirect political democracy), but eventually it turned out to be a political project of the communists for acquiring and maintaining economic power in society. Armed with a 'revolutionary Marxist theory', socialist doctrine very strictly condemned private ownership, market competition, capital and the profit motive for causing exploitation and false political democracy in society. It strove for collectivist political action (dictatorship of the proletariat), nationalisation of enterprises (state-owned and/or social property), reallocation of social wealth and a powerful state carrying out centrally planned management in enterprises.

Socialist ideology and practice denied the two fundamental institutions of a free market system: political participation (pluralist multi-party democracy, a legal state and the freedom of citizens) and the entrepreneurial initiative (private property, capital and market competition). As market institutions (capital market, labour market, market competition) were not recognised by socialism, and also the informative and allocation role of prices was not renounced, a rational economic calculation was not

possible. In short, the theory of economic calculation shows that in socialist communities economic calculation is impossible (Mises 1979). Without
the striving of entrepreneurs for profit, without effective market competition
and price system, the successful functioning of the whole market mechanism
is not possible. This is, of course, an abstract theoretical approach which
turned up in the famous discussion of Mises, Hayek and Lange in the
1930s (Lavoir 1985) as a hypothesis that will be dealt with in the discussion
of the Yugoslav case. The argument is that a socialist economy can never
be as efficient as a capitalist one because there exists a fundamental contradiction between ethical principles and market institutions. All experiments
in designing 'market models of socialism' (for instance Lange's model of
artificial markets for the means of production and allocation of investments carried out by the state) show that it is quite impossible to organise
the economy rationally and to democratise political relations in a society if
there are no private ownership, no markets for means of production and
no market competition or entrepreneurship. Socialist utopias were not
able to find replacements for market institutions, but the liberal myth of
free markets, private property rights and entrepreneurial motivation cannot satisfy all social needs and interests (Brus 1985).

The process of economic deregulation and political liberalisation calls
for special 'recapitalisation of socialism' because the 'post-socialist society'
cannot (does not) differ very much from the so-called social market
economies of Western Europe, either in the economic or the political
sense (Kovač, 1990). From that point of view, the post-socialist society can
continue to exist only as a social policy of a legally elected democratic government. Such a social policy of market deregulation and liberalisation
should release the creativity of the people, develop entrepreneurship and
with the rule of law provide legal safety, political freedom (civil society
and the state) and, with a social policy of redistribution, a greater social
justice.

Even if it is assumed, however, that the above changes become reality
(and from a politically ideological view they are not questioned by the
majority of the population in socialist countries), there is still the question
of 'how to do it', 'how to normalise socialist society politically and economically'. In this field Yugoslavia has much theoretical and historical experience
(self-management economy since 1950), but in the historical circumstances of today it has neither political will nor wisdom to be able to utilise
the experiences, either for its own sake or for the sake of others.

Economic analysis of self-managed enterprises and social ownership in the post-war period

The post-war economic development of Yugoslavia can be divided into
five periods:

1. 1945–53—In the first period the 'revolutionary Marxist theory' asserted that private property and markets led to social anarchy and maintained capitalist relations of exploitation. Therefore they had to be replaced with centrally planned enterprises and state-owned property.
2. 1953–63—In the second period ownership was gradually handed over to workers' collectives in enterprises and they paid the state a special rent at a determined price for state capital (interest on business fund and/or equity of the enterprise).
3. 1963–76—In this period collective self-management started to develop, workers were given the right to manage joint income, interest on business funds was abolished and investment functions were taken over by enterprises instead of by the state itself.
4. 1976–87—There was a tendency to develop and bring into effect Marx's vision of 'associated socialism' with integral self-management, social ownership, distribution of income according to work performed, social consultation and self-managed agreement—making enterprises the places where workers' self-management was developed.
5. 1987–90—The fifth period was the period of radical market reform, which is characterised by the introduction of the privatisation strategy for social ownership, autonomy of enterprises, capital and labour markets, and management based on capital and labour (participation).

After 1945 a strong business fund was established as a result of 'revolutionary economic measures' of the communist regime such as agricultural reform and nationalisation. In the Constitution of 1963 this fund was simply called 'general national property, which is managed by the state with the help of state-owned enterprises'. The economy was organised as an enormous hierarchically managed, state-owned cartel (*Hilferding*). Nationalised state-owned property was transformed into a specific socialist ownership property category—the business fund.

An important turning-point for the development of property and enterprise relations came at the beginning of the 1950s when workers' self-management and market economy were introduced (a new act on enterprises—1950) and state-owned property was gradually transformed into social property (Horvat 1971). Thus social ownership was identified as common ownership by workers' collectives and/or work organisations by which social resources were managed. The socialist state itself determined its utility price (interest on the business fund) instead of the capital market. In the 1963 Constitution it was clearly stated (Article 15) that the work organisation was a legal entity and had the economic right to use social resources. The state was not the direct owner of enterprises but the basic functions of an enterprise were still controlled by it (investments, recruitment of managers, covering losses, setting up and closing down enterprises, etc.).

Until the mid-1960s enterprises were paying interest on the business fund and thus accumulating state capital. With the Amendments to the Constitution of 1971 and the new Constitution of 1974, an indirect form of ownership was introduced and enterprises were given the right independently to dispose of their joint income (investments included). We can divide the post-war years of 'socialist development' into three periods:

1st period   state-owned property → state-owned enterprises

2nd period   state-owned property
                    | |
                    capital prices, state-owned capital investment
                    |
                    workers' collective

3rd period   social property → free social labour → workers'
                    collectives

In the 1970s communist governments wanted to realise Marx's vision of socialism, so, with the new act on enterprises (Associated Labour Act), the following changes were introduced:

1. remodelling and decentralisation of enterprises into organisations of associated labour;
2. democratisation of self-management in enterprises based on the principle of one worker, one vote;
3. non-market association of enterprises through social agreements and self-management agreements.

In the system of freely associated labour the traditional enterprise does not exist. BOAL (basic organisation of associated labour) is an organisational form in which workers realise their self-management rights and socialist self-management relations (the profit motive is replaced with responsibility based on solidarity between BOALs. Business functions in the market are usually taken over by work organisations, which in fact are self-managed enterprises (Prašnikar and Prašnikar 1986).

Decision-making in a self-managed enterprise is very complex and consists of three institutions: (1) Workers' self-management of business decisions (workers' council, workers' assembly); (2) management carried out by managers; (3) indirect management by the state.

The business policy of a self-managed enterprise differs from a traditional market enterprise as follows:

1. In a self-managed enterprise the total number of employed workers is

much above average (low capital price, employment security, lack of competition, political aims are achieved easily).
2. Enterprises are more oriented towards capital-intensive investments (high income taxes for workers, no taxes on technological rents, low capital price).
3. In big enterprises average costs and extra payments are determined by price policy, prices are administratively determined in cycles or they are liberalised, enterprises usually respond to market changes in a 'perverse' way (higher prices—lower supply) (Prašnikar and Svejner 1988).
4. Incomes of workers vary from enterprise to enterprise and differences are much greater than in developed market economies (undeveloped capital market and labour market, undeveloped competition, limited entrance of new enterprises) (Estrin, Svejner and Moore 1988).
5. Maximisation of personal incomes and common consumption are part of the business objectives of the enterprise, while investments are financed by banks or partly by the financial structure of the enterprise itself, but hardly ever with the financial resources of other enterprises (self-managed economy is a credit economy, responsibility of owners of social property is not clearly determined).
6. The size of enterprise is above average, market concentration is extremely high, three-quarters of markets have oligopolistic or monopolistic features (big enterprises have monopolistic power in planning and development, they are centres of political power).
7. There are great regional differences in productivity between enterprises in developed and undeveloped regions of Yugoslavia (developed areas: Slovenia, Croatia, Vojvodina, part of Serbia).

Permanent financial resources are not available to self-managed enterprises. Since there is no real owner who would protect creditors, the government always intervenes in business decisions concerning the financial state of enterprises. Various forms of interference (managers are chosen and determined by the state), programmes of readjustment and solvency, as well as opening up new enterprises are evidence that even in this case, we have to talk about a modified form of state-owned enterprise. Enterprises are automatically financed by the banking system (NB, commercial banks), but money is never repaid at its real value (negative interests rates). Commercial banks cover the losses of enterprises in the name of the state and thus a vicious circle of 'soft budget constraints' (Kornai 1986) in a socialist self-managed enterprise is finally closed. The efficiency of a self-managed enterprise is below average.

We know from the theory of worker-managed market socialism and Yugoslav practice that a worker-managed enterprise of the Yugoslav type differs from a traditional market-oriented enterprise in at least three crucial elements by which economic efficiency is also determined. These are:

1. Social ownership prevents the assets of an enterprise from being formed in such way as to be the subject of trade (enterprise as a commodity) and to be financed by continual long-term resources (social ownership has a permanent credit relationship either to the state until 1971 with interest on the business fund or to commercial banks).
2. The risk for business decisions is always borne by the banking system on behalf of the state. Decision-making of workers and managers is, therefore, always ineffective and irresponsible ('soft budget constraints', bad lack of financial discipline as the logical foundation of the social ownership concept).
3. Self-management inhibits efficient workers' control of business activity and management of an enterprise; workers' interests are not linked enough with ownership, profit-making or loss of employment to make decisions economically rational.

This means that for worker-managed enterprises of the Yugoslav type a precise definition of social ownership and the functioning of the enterprise from a financial and entrepreneurial view is of great importance. Yet, by worker-managed market socialism three basic restrictions were imposed: (1) socialist self-management excluded a labour market; (2) socialism excluded a capital market; and (3) distribution of income according to work performed excluded the appropriation of property.

Every property model needs to answer four fundamental questions related to business activity. Who is the subject of property (who has a title to property)? Who takes the risks in business? Who makes the profit (who shares the profit)? And by whom is business controlled? In the social property model the formal subject of ownership is 'society', but in fact the owner cannot be defined (state, workers' collective, workers). Business risk is taken by the state (long term) and by enterprises (short term). Profit is appropriated by employees (state protects ownership with depreciation). Control over enterprises is exercised through informal political pressures or even through direct state intervention when a firm goes bankrupt.

This means that in a social property model traditional enterprises and market institutions are not possible. Worker-managed market socialism is management-oriented and not property-oriented. Its starting-points are not capital and property of the enterprise but labour and the right to social resources. As such, economy is not property-oriented. There are also no permanent investors of capital in enterprises. Self-managers only 'associate' labour so resources can be obtained from the state either as 'gifts' or 'loans'. Furthermore, management of an enterprise is not defined precisely enough so the role of the state, managers or workers in management is not clearly defined either.

New requirements for economic reform and privatisation strategy

In the second half of the 1980s the Yugoslav authorities began to believe that the period of 'cultural revolution' (extraordinary politicisation and ideologisation of the state) in the 1970s was a political mistake and that a market economy, greater freedom of enterprises, a greater role for ownership and entrepreneurship, were the key to increased efficiency of the economy. The economic commission of the federal government made out (1988) a document of changes of all the basic parts of the economic system. Among them were the most important transformations of the 'organisation of associated labour' into enterprise and of social ownership as 'non-ownership' into 'social capital'.

In 1989 the experience of applying the law on enterprises showed some new opportunities and alternative approaches, which could be put into two categories:

1. The financial approach advocates a capital-based organisation of enterprises and financial consolidation of the economy (diversification of financial institutions, holding companies, shareholding, stock exchange, venture capital institutions, institutional investors, such as insurance companies, pension funds, etc.).
2. The entrepreneurial approach advocates the efficient entrepreneurial use of 'social property' by different entrepreneurial groups (internal entrepreneurship, profit-sharing programmes, programmes of workers' shares, management buy-outs, etc.).

Both approaches are complementary and call for mutual co-ordination. Financial consolidation of an enterprise does not necessarily mean that the enterprise is market-efficient, and vice-versa. Without 'cleaning up' the financial affairs of an enterprise, any kind of entrepreneurial restructuring is absurd (Nuti 1989). Neither is possible without well-developed market institutions, especially capital and labour markets, markets for entrepreneurial expertise and open market competition, all of which promote the independence of an enterprise in the market and employees' market initiative (Vahčič 1989).

The first difficulty lies in the fact that the capital and labour markets are incompatible with the basic institution of the present system. The labour market is incompatible with the concept of self-management, while the capital market is opposed to social ownership. Organising the labour market is an easier task because it has no strong negative associations with some past institutional misconceptions of socialist economics, and contains at the same time forms of participatory democracy which could be similar to our methods of self-management. The basic requirement for organising labour markets is for the formation of free and autonomous trade unions which would represent workers interests (agreement on wage rates, degree of supervision of employees, employees' insurance and working conditions, social protection in case of job loss, legal protection, etc.) as opposed to the state (federal, republican and municipal administration), and management organised in chambers of commerce or business groupings.

The capital market, particularly in the form of securities, has in the short term no great future for at least two reasons. Since Yugoslavia is, in the political sense, an exceptionally unstable country, the risk of capital transactions (joint ventures) is greatly increased. On the other hand, the structure of current financial sources is linked primarily with commercial banks, and it is therefore more realistic to expect that entrepreneurial finance could become 'normalised' between enterprises and banks (a similar linkage, for instance, exists in the Federal Republic of Germany, but not, however, in Britain where financial transactions are conducted primarily in the capital market). This does not, of course, mean that the necessary financial institutions should not be set up as soon as possible. It would be unrealistic, however, to expect that this could provide a solution to the social property model.

Economic analysts and reform strategists in socialist countries usually overlook an exceptionally important aspect of the capital market, i.e. the valuation of an enterprise's assets (equity) (Economic Reforms 1989). Determining the value of assets of an enterprise is of crucial significance because it involves cleaning up the enterprise's portfolio and establishing the titular owner of the property. Yugoslav enterprises have so far been assessing the value of their business funds on the basis of accounting records. Such a method of obtaining information does not reveal the market (real) value of an enterprise. An enterprise must first become a commodity, the object of exchange (of buying and selling), before its value can be ascertained. This will be based on its future profits (profitability) and not on its 'historical' accounts.

In a market economy, with well-developed share ownership and long-term capital markets (primary and secondary markets), the value of the assets is best reflected in the market value of shares. However, neither share capital nor the securities market represent real prerequisites in Yugoslavia, and it is therefore more realistic to expect an enterprise to be valued on the basis of an assessment of its future profit, competition, business risk, technological development and market 'goodwill'.

If there is neither a well-developed capital market nor a legitimate enterprise owner, valuation of the enterprise can be made by three competitive institutions: the state, represented by special federal, republican or municipal financial institutions (agencies); the enterprises, by their own or by specialised consultancy organisations; while the third institution could be a commercial bank. There is also a real limit to the possible valuation of assets. If valuation is too low, there is a danger of the enterprise being bought up by a third person. If it it too high, dividends for owners of the capital would increase abnormally. A realistic assessment of an enterprise's assets is, of course, connected with cleaning up its existing portfolio (abandoning unprofitable projects and business units, changing the source of finance, converting long-term credits into equities, short-term credits into long-term, writing off interest) and reducing the surplus workforce. This process represents only another way of setting up capital and labour markets at the level of an enterprise which determine its position in relation to the economic system as a whole.

If the valuation of the 'real' assets of an enterprise (business fund) is known, we have in business practice various methods of the privatisation of social property, which resemble some entrepreneurial strategies in countries with well-developed market economies. We shall describe here only four proposals which have very often been the subject of study by our enterprises, where they were restructured into entrepreneurial firms on the basis of the law on enterprises. It should, however, be pointed out, that all these options have been used more to resolve the problem of social ownership than to achieve real financial consolidation of enterprises.

A. The step taken most frequently, at least by Slovene composite enterprise, was the formation of holding companies. A holding company is a joint financial enterprise, formed by firms to conduct joint financial operations and facilitate their ventures on the capital market. The main task of a holding company is to raise capital, sort out the financial portfolios of its subsidiaries, decapitalise firms, buy up and incorporate firms, and conduct management on a financial basis. Our 'Yugo-holding' system has other tasks: it serves the redistribution of 'social property' and capital-oriented organisation of enterprises.

The entire operation is fairly simple.

1. Self-management enterprises form a holding company (apex firm), transfer to it their business funds (the percentage of the transfer is a matter of agreement by them) and manage it.
2. The holding company forms subsidiaries by reciprocated capital and controls them (the percentage of the transfer is again a matter of agreement). Such a double financial operation (cross-ownership) transforms anonymous social property into nominal property and creates a certain 'financial federation' (and why not, since our political federations are going under!), which exist in the financial structures of corporations in advanced market countries (the Japanese *keiretsu* is nothing else but a form of such a cross-ownership model, with some additional formal and informal agreements among the firms).

The shortcoming of this approach is that it is confined to financial operations, which creates, *ex lege*, for shareholders a work collective (a holding company is either a limited company or a public limited company) and transforms social ownership into collective ownerships, without making any changes at the level of an enterprise. Or, conversely, changes at the enterprise level, in the form of managerial and control functions, become politically problematical because they demand that social power be redistributed between the holding company and subsidiaries below (a holding company manages enterprises), without the real strength of the subsidiaries or the method of redistributing assets between them and the holding company being clear (there is a discrepancy between the balance sheet of the actual state of affairs and the balance sheet of success; the economic strength of an enterprise does not correspond to the value of the business fund as the object of redistribution and management). Because of the unclear conditions in which they are set up (the real value of transferable property is unknown), holding companies have often caused a firm's 'political' disintegration (loss of consensus between managerial groups, managers and workers), legal break-up or the loosening of bonds between firms which, after all, is not the purpose for which they have combined their capital.

B. The second proposal proceeds from the opposite assumption. Social property is not collectivised but individualised. It belongs to the employed workers and the business fund is literally the result of their 'past labour'. This creates 'workers' shares', into which the business fund is divided on the basis of various criteria (average personal income over the past ten years, permanency of employment, past investment and renouncing of consumption). Such shares would be transferable on a restricted basis (highly taxed if sold; various ways of prohibiting property from being taken out of an enterprise). Despite the fact that this is a very popular model in the ideology of self-management, it has serious drawbacks:

1. The business fund represents first and foremost an 'historical category', the growth and size of which depend primarily on the distorted economic system, on market conditions, and only, in the ultimate analysis, on workers' labour itself.
2. It is technically impossible to determine the contributions made by individual workers (a particular problem is the relationship between present and past employees). In applying this model we should not resolve the issue of social justice (moreover, we should most likely create a new type of 'social *rentier*' and lead society into a social revolution).
3. 'Workers' property' does not resolve the problem of management for it again puts the worker in a dual relationship—as a worker and proprietor. This is extremely problematical with respect to risk-bearing and control of management in an enterprise.

C. The only possibility, therefore, of introducing share capital, including 'workers' shares', is their operation in the market. An enterprise can, of course, offer shares first to its own managers (management buy-out) or to its workers on special terms, i.e. at a value lower than their market value (this is the practice of British privatisation). It can, together with the state, give loans to workers to purchase shares (this is the practice of the American ESOP—Employees' Share Option Plan). Workers receive the paid-out portion of profit in the form of shares etc. However, even the property model of market shares contains some questionable elements. If there is no ownership concept of social property, we do not know the owner, i.e. who the seller is, whose job it is to buy and whose to sell, how to determine prices in an underdeveloped capital market, etc. The legislation on ownership should at least stipulate that all social enterprises are, by law, for sale (property is part of legal business) and that everybody—enterprises, banks, financial institutions, Yugoslavs, foreigners and non-financial institutions can purchase socially-owned enterprises or securities at their market values.

D. Lastly, there is also a fourth proposal, which looks for the titular owner of social property outside the enterprise in the relationship between the state and enterprises. The role of the title-holder of social property is taken over by special financial institutions with a differentiated and democratically organised ownership structure (such ideal 'social' share 'capital' is represented, for instance, by pension funds, within the framework of the transformed pension insurance communities). 'Democratic financial institutions' fulfil some important conditions concerning the normalisation of entrepreneurial finance. They are not the state, and as titular owners of business funds they are outside the enterprise and have no managerial rights which could become contentious on account of the 'historical socialist heritage' of the business fund. Thus, enterprises transfer their business funds to democratic financial institutions for preference shares which bear dividends. The enterprise retains autonomy of management. Contributions to pension funds are reduced by the amount of the dividend, while the business fund, as anonymous social capital, disappears from the enterprise's balance sheet. When cleaning up the portfolios of enterprises (determining the business fund's real value), successful enterprises will take on the debts of unsuccessful ones (debt–equity swap mechanism), just as special financial institutions (investment trusts), which convert debts into their risk capital, could also do.

This proposal is debatable, primarily because of the universal belief that entrepreneurial activity of enterprises does not necessarily have to change with financial consolidation. Moreover, there is a real danger of the transfer of the business fund to a 'social holding company' becoming the object of extensive financial speculation and manipulation, particularly by financially unsuccessful enterprises. No less significant is the comment that such an operation does not in fact change anything at the enterprise level, because 'democratic financial institutions' do not thereby acquire any managerial rights. Of course, the entire existing procedure of reforming the capital base of an enterprise (holding company, workers' shares, market shares) on the basis of 'social ownership' thus becomes nonsensical. It is, furthermore, illogical why the transfer of the business fund on this basis should not be considered cross-ownership, similar to the corporations' own shares (treasury stock in the American corporation law), which carries no managerial voting rights or dividends.

It would, therefore, be better to set up public holding companies with their own capital, like the well-known Italian IRI (Istituto per la Ricostruzione Industriale). Public enterprises (enterprises with state property) and the state would form a joint holding company, which would be their main shareholder, their financial decision centre (drawing up investment plans and raising finance), and which would influence the selection of leading businessmen in enterprises. In the last three years they have also been involved in an interesting privatisation by providing facilities for private capital investment, which has made mixing private and public capital flexible and provided the opportunity of ascertaining the best enterprise portfolios in their grouping.

Thus we have arrived at the basic problem of how to change the social ownership structure. It contains at least four 'axioms':

1. As there is no universal solution, only a gradual and selective solution of the problem is possible (limited and complementary use of all the four potential solutions is feasible).
2. Formation of capital and labour markets is the starting-point; however, without a fundamental valuation of the assets of an enterprise and cleaning up of its financial portfolio as well as the introduction of a sound employment policy, social ownership cannot be abolished.
3. There are only public and private sectors, and social property should therefore be allocated to one or the other sector (or even better, abolished).
4. There must be, therefore, a political and economic programme of 'nationalising' self-managing enterprises, within the framework of public corporations and their holding groupings (like the IRI) or a 'privatisation' programme in the form of internal decentralisation (internal entrepreneurship) of enterprises with different methods of individualising ownership rights (management buy-out, workers' shares, market shares, cross-ownership, spin-off).

Social ownership is a socialist relic, which except for communist authorities, has no economic or legal *raison d'être*. However, despite the failure of the political and economic concept of socialism and the decline of communist power, the economic and technical problem of 'normalising' the socialist economy by transforming it into market economy is great. To experiment in this sphere, with or without communists, could be catastrophic for the economy, which will operate anyway in exceptionally unstable political conditions. Since extensive external funding of economic reform by European capital cannot be expected (Yugoslavia will not, in all likelihood, be considered in the first cycle of EC financial aid intended for socialist Central Europe), there is little scope for real reform of the ownership system. In such an unenviable situation, the government should at least give enterprises a clear legal framework of their future development strategy. Enterprises themselves should find some kind of solution. The state will still have its fiscal system and mechanisms of indirect intervention in these spontaneous economic developments. If political authority is incapable of directing the state, it should at least enable managers and workers in enterprises to do so.

References

Brus, W., 1985. 'Socialism—feasible and viable', *New Left Review*, no. 153.

Economic Reforms, 1989. *Economic Reforms in the European Centrally Planned Economies*, Economic Commission for Europe, Wiener Institut für Internationale Wirtschaftvergleiche, United Nations, Vienna and New York.

Estrin, S., Svejner J., Moore R., 1988. 'Market imperfection, labour management and earnings differentials in developing countries: theory and economic evidence from Yugoslavia', *Quarterly Journal of Economics*, no. 2.

Horvat, B., 1971. 'Yugoslav economic policy in the postwar period: problems, ideas, institutional developments', *American Economic Review*, no. 61.

Kovač, B., 1990. Rekviem za socializem, *Državna založba Slovenije*.

Kornai, J., 1986. 'The soft budget constraints', *Kyklos*, no. 39.

Lavoir, D., 1985. *Rivalry and Control Planning: The Socialist Calculation Debate Reconsidered*, Cambridge University Press.

Mises, L., 1979. *Socialism. An Economic and Sociological Analysis*, Liberty Classics.

Nuti, M., 1989. 'Remonetisation and capital markets in the reform of centrally planned economies', *European Economic Review*, no. 33.

Prašnikar, J., Prašnikar, V., 1988. 'The Yugoslav selfmanaged firm in historical perspective', *Economic and Industrial Democracy*, no. 7.

Prašnikar, J., Svejner, J., 1988. Economic Behaviour of Yugoslav Firm, in *Advances in the Economic Analyses of Participatory and Labour-Managed Firms*, no. 3.

Vahčič, A., 1989. 'Capital markets, management takeovers and creation of new firms', *European Economic Review*, no. 33.

Further reading

Bajt, A., 1986. 'Economic growth and factor substitution: What happened to the Yugoslav miracle? Some comments', *Economic Journal*, 96.

Kornai, J., 1990. *The Road to a Free Economy*, Norton, New York.

Prašnikar, J., 1990. *Workers Participation in Development Countries*, Westview Press.

Sacs, S.R., 1983. *Self-management and Efficiency, Large Corporation in Yugoslavia*, Allen & Unwin.

PART IV
SOCIAL JUSTICE AND SOCIAL POLICY

INTRODUCTION

James Simmie

The twin legitimation bases of Marxist-inspired communist regimes rest on claims to generate industrial economic growth and social equality in the distribution of the resulting resources. Characteristically, as in Yugoslavia, they have fallen short of the achievement of both aims. In Part III we saw the relative failure of the Communist party to generate economic growth in Yugoslavia comparable to that of other Southern European market economies. In Part IV we shall see how it has also failed to achieve one of the central objectives in Marxist theory, namely, significant increases in social equality. It was assumed that these would result automatically in conditions of economic growth, social ownership of the means of production and their self-management by labour.

In Part IV we see how the 'technical' abolition of social classes, in the Marxist sense, by the abolition of private property, does not automatically lead to greater social equality. In the first place it does not change other forms of social stratification such as status groups and the party. In the second place it prevents the development of policies which could ameliorate social inequality by denying its very existence.

In the three chapters of Part IV, Barbara Verlič-Dekleva discusses why Yugoslav social policy has been so limited in its effects on equality; Pavel Gantar and Srna Mandič illustrate the lack of social equality in housing allocations; and Ognjen Čaldarović looks at urban social inequality. Taken together the three analyses show how inequality has persisted and even been re-created under self-managed Yugoslav communism.

Barbara Verlič-Dekleva addresses the phenomenon of the overlap between economic and social policy. She points out that although human and social equality were major objectives of the post-war transformation of Yugoslavia, they have not been achieved in practice. One of the main reasons for this appears to be that much of the burden for social security has been placed on the economy and within individual enterprises. Workers with jobs in enterprises cannot be fired and this forms the basis of their social security.

In addition to this mechanism, all employees and enterprises have to contribute to common funds for the provision of social services. These funds are insufficient to prevent scarcities and so inequalities of distribution re-emerge. The higher social status groups accumulate privileges in the acquisition of social services.

The management of the social funds and their allocation in conditions of scarcity, has itself become a new source of inequality. It has led to the emergence of what has been called a 'red bourgeoisie'. Urban gatekeepers are alive and powerful in Yugoslavia!

These social security mechanisms are not universal. There is large-scale unemployment in Yugoslavia, as shown in Part III. The unemployed do not benefit from the security of permanent employment in enterprises. Social funds are scarce and many unemployed are too far down the queues for them to receive any benefits. Thus large sections of the population are not covered by any form of social security at all.

Two strategies for overcoming the lack of work have been adopted. The first is emigration, particularly to Austria, Germany and other West European countries needing cheap labour. Such workers usually have no social security cover in their adopted countries, but at least they have work.

The second strategy is the development of a 'grey' economy. This involves extensive moonlighting and contribution evasion. It is so pervasive that it prevents serious contemplation of changing working hours to match those of Western Europe. According to Barbara Verlič-Dekleva, it affects some 20 per cent of the entire Yugoslav work-force.

Yugoslav social policy has not, therefore, been a means to the reduction of social inequalities. After nearly half a century of the communist experiment major inequalities persist between regions, workers, those without work and those confined to the 'grey' economy.

Among the basic necessities of life, few exceed housing in their importance for the quality of everyday life. Pavel Gantar and Srna Mandič examine the effects of communist housing policies and their contribution to social equality. Housing equality has been a primary tenet of Marxist/Leninist-inspired Communist party political programmes. As a result it has become one of the archetypal social services which socialists of many factions believe should be collectively provided. In Yugoslavia some collective provision and funding has indeed been made.

Nevertheless, housing provision in Yugoslavia holds many surprises for Western observers. One surprise is the connection between large construction firms and the state. In Britain this contributed to the construction of unpopular and unnecessary high-rise apartment blocks. In Yugoslavia the story is much the same. High-rise blocks are to be seen even in comparatively rural communes.

Even so, familiar shortages in housing supply have persisted. The formal construction sector is unable to supply enough housing. Investment primacy has been given to industrialisation as opposed to urbanisation. As a result urban housing is scarce, particularly in and around industrial centres. Workers have therefore been left to build their own accommodation. A large, informal self-build sector has developed in most major cities. Such initially shanty suburbs accommodate anything up to 20 per cent of their populations.

Serious housing inequalities have therefore emerged between those in the more desirable social housing and those in self-build accommodation. There are also 'unofficial' inequalities in the allocation of social housing itself. These arise because that type of housing is very scarce and is allocated according to a series of criteria associated with need and 'merit'. In the trade-off between need and 'merit' the latter seems to have become increasingly important in allocation. The result has been that social housing is allocated disproportionately to higher social status groups.

One major reason for this, identified by Pavel Gantar and Srna Mandič, is the fact that social housing has become a form of employment benefit, rather like the company car in Britain. Much of it is allocated through enterprises according to the perceived value of employees to the enterprise. Not only has there been competition within enterprises but also for jobs in those which have the most housing to allocate. These are invariably political and government organisations, so that political, economic, intellectual and cultural élites have acquired the greatest proportion of social housing.

The final surprise for Western observers is that about 80 per cent of the housing stock is still privately owned. This is primarily because of the continuation of private ownership in rural areas. This is partly because of a lack of social housing outside urban areas and also the persistence of workers with both agricultural and industrial jobs.

In urban areas, Ognjen Čaldarović shows that inequalities in location are added to those of housing quality to produce further social inequality in cities. He takes as his starting-point the assumption that equality of living conditions for everybody is not found anywhere. Nevertheless, social stratification and residential segregation are another set of phenomena which are supposed to be abolished by definition with the establishment of a revolutionary Marxist society. This assumption has inhibited analysis of such phenomena in Marxist societies because, like much of the information contained in this volume, it undermines the basis of Marxist theory. Consequently, most analyses which could cast some light on the question of social justice were deformed and marginalised.

Nevertheless, Ognjen Čaldarović reports research findings which show first that different social status groups were in possession of different housing rights. Some 16 per cent of workers, for example, compared with 57 per cent of politicians, were shown to have rights to social housing. Second, housing quality varied in about the same proportion. Third, in

Zagreb, at least, higher social status groups were found concentrated disproportionately in central areas while workers were more often concentrated on the periphery. At present this remains one of the more striking contrasts between cities in market as compared with collective economies. The latter appear, however, to be different rather than more equal.

For most practical purposes, the abolition of social classes defined according to Marx has not removed social stratification in communist societies such as Yugoslavia. As far as most people's everyday lives are concerned, social status and party distinctions continue to be the basis of significant social and material inequalities.

7 IMPLICATIONS OF ECONOMIC CHANGE TO SOCIAL POLICY

Barbara Verlič-Dekleva

Introduction

Yugoslavia is in the process of changing the regulation of its economy. The basis of this change is strategically not questioned. It consists of rational, more efficient and market-oriented instruments (Marković's programme, from 1989 president of the Yugoslav government). It is not clear how we are prepared to cope with the social impacts of such a change and redefine the specifics of our social policy. The main problem is a dramatic increase in unemployment, combined with a lack of social security.

One of the main features of the socialist system has been the overlapping of the economy and social policy, both controlled by political ideology. This 'compact system' developed a substantial level of redistribution of resources (the principle of mandatory solidarity) and poor economic results. Redistribution is accomplished through national budget funds, through manipulation of accounting[1] and 'political' management.

Since we hope to improve economic efficiency, that implies separation of social policy from the economy. The problem is how to redefine the former. At the moment the change from communist ideology (political change which has introduced a multi-party system) is particularly painful and regional or administrative decentralisation of decision-making is increasing.

Thousands of workers are out of work. Young people have no or few prospects. There is no guarantee of social security. Real personal incomes have decreased since 1979. In 1986 their value was worth less than in 1970 (Delo 16.11.1984). According to estimates 30–60 per cent of families with children in some regions have less than the minimal living standards or no reserves left in case of need. 45.4 per cent of families in Yugoslavia are occasionally short of money for food or other essential expenses. Fifty per cent of families are living in sub-standard housing[2] (*Quality of Life* research = *QL*, 1988/9, Boh, Tomc).

My intention here is to analyse the socialist concept of social policy and explain why it is, as it is. Besides values, goals and instruments of social policy, I shall stress typical connections between politics (political ideology of the communists) and the economic sector of society, and the relation of the two to social policy in Yugoslavia.

'Soc-realism' of social policy

The concept of social policy we are going to discuss deals with the well-being, minimum standard of living and social security of the whole population, rather than with the disabled, elderly or children (wider and narrow meaning of the term, Titmuss 1973). The problem is twofold and is manifested in the basis of social security and the level of social services available.

I. The indubitable fact in most socialist countries is the overlapping and interrelation of the economy and social policy, within a system where government seeks to minimise negative social effects inside the economic sector itself. That implies government interference with political and normative interventions in the economy in order to resolve social objective (full employment, social security, housing, etc.). Such objectives are important bases of 'socialist' legitimation. In so far as economists persuade us of the ideological regulation of the economy, it is important to stress the consequences of intermingling social policy and the economy. Social security of the population is based on 'permanent' employment where labour employment is not economic but rather a social category and economic investment is a political decision.

The socialist state undermines or denies the role of an independent concept of social security *per se* (on the basis of citizenship, for example), and with the pursuit of an active social policy itself. The first effect of that has been a population 'push' to social sector employment, for example, especially by women. Slovenia has one of the highest rates of women employed in Europe. Of the women aged between 15 and 64, 71.6 per cent were employed in 1984 (*Statistic Yearbook* 1988:455/7). (OECD countries for 1982 reveal 72.7 per cent of women employed.) In Yugoslavia in 1987 38.4 per cent of those employed in the social sector were women. Those who failed to gain such employment were confined to marginal, restricted private sector employment (with negative stigma until recently) or emigration.

II. Within the programmes of social activities (like child-care, education, health care and housing), rigid standardisation of services, spread of administration, low productivity and higher cost of such programmes is increasing. All that neglects the actual demands and needs of different groups of the population. Research results reveal inadequate levels of choice or quality of services, which are also too expensive. The problem remains of how to persuade people to use and pay for them. This is done by the strict ideological control of institutions and the prevention of private or civil initiative in organising alternative solutions.

Social organisations follow the logic of expansion and complexity. For that, more professional staff, more coordination and resources are needed. Their monopoly position encourages them to do so as long as the state does not reduce the finances (due to poor economic results), which decreases the social standards of the households. Despite this, the state does not change its policy. It does not allow individual or collective initiative, which could mobilise additional resources. (Informativni Bilten, Svetlik 1987, pp. 19, 20).

Instead of taking an active part in the reconception and co-ordination of programmes, the socialist state (CP)—in order to keep power—maintains the institutions, despite the fact that they neither produce adequate services nor assure quality. Public opinion research from 1987 provides some illustrations. In 1978 only 2.2 per cent of the Slovene population thought they had lower living standards than five years previously; in 1982 this share increased to 29.1 per cent, and in 1986 to 61 per cent. In 1987, 62.2 per cent of Slovenes had no possibility of any kind of savings (QL 1988, Tomc).

It is evident that ideological obstacles and a need for social and political control make a socialist state dogmatic rather than pragmatic. Such features define the limits of its transformation, which should not threaten the monopoly of the CP. Since the government needs to do something, it proposes normative reforms, which are not changing the content of public activities, but rather the forms of their organisation.

Shift from state planning to the market

The latest reforms (December 1989) introduced in both sectors, the economy and public services, the inevitable tendency to market, profit-oriented and more efficient organisation as a response to the general crisis. Such decisions are increasingly counter-related to social goals. Thus the failure of political planning of the economy challenges its productivity, destroying the basis of social security for workers.

Social security built into permanent employment increases the inability of economic management to change the labour and professional structure of organisations, which may lead to bankruptcy.[3] The workers cannot change their jobs since there is no labour market, nor is there any social policy and security outside the economy. Nothing less than active and independent social policy would enable economic change to happen, increasing profitability and thus enabling the restructuring of the economy to be pursued.

To demand restructuring of the economy, introduction of market rationality, without the formation of independent and active social policy, will provoke social conflicts. It is a crisis of the socialist state's functions which we are discussing. Instead of taking the responsibility for adequate provision and financing of public services, the government prefers to hold on to power.

The present critical situation, in which the economic decline and delays in radical change are consuming all spare resources, reveals the contradictions of existing social policy. Decreasing social standards lead to the instability of the socialist state.[4] It makes political change inevitable and with that the monopoly ideological position of the Communist party must end. What are the instruments, enabling such a system to function and what are its main features? Why is it impossible to reform it in order to assure minimum economic and human standards?[5]

The genesis of the 'present situation' in social policy

After the Second World War, together with other reforms following the Soviet example, it was taken for granted (as a result of the critique of 'bourgeois society') that we needed a radical transformation of society. In this project, the social rights and obligations of workers were of prime importance. Social policy thus became a legitimation of such a project. Ružica (1987 p.13) remembers that such ideas were founded on goals to achieve human equality and social justice rather than civil human rights.

The first stage of the operation was the redistribution of land, housing and food during the years after the Second World War.[6] Social security of workers was effected by the constitutional right to work, to housing, personal prosperity and security (education, retirement, health care, etc.). The workers could not be fired. The right to use a socially owned flat is permanent, cheap and transferable to other members of the family. Education is free. Benefits are fixed and controlled by the state, enabling redistribution among economic, regional and social sectors, from agriculture to industry, from the countryside to new industrial centres, and from urban centres to new construction, etc.

Additionally, local authorities control production and producers, determining the extent of public consumption. A constant shortage of some goods makes people work and spend time in order to satisfy very basic needs. It is an efficient means of 'social control' of behaviour and lifestyle. Basic needs of the population, both individual and collective, are 'socialised' by forming common funds (with obligations for all employees and firms to make contributions that are not refundable) for education, culture, infrastructure, housing, health, retirement, etc.

Because of bad administration and the scarcity of resources, waiting lists, priorities and planning regulations result in the actual uneven or inadequate provision of social services. A supply, not found on 'the market', transfers its own byways to the 'customers', thus fostering inequalities and privileges. For example, special pensions, housing and vacation facilities provided a better living standard for the important party personnel. Waiting time for social housing for the average household might take a decade or more. It may never happen at all. Self-provision is thus necessary, explaining a wide range of 'black', illegal housing construction among other private forms of provision.

Quality of Life research[7] provides some more illustrations. Results reveal the level of public and social facilities available at different locations to different groups of the population. The allocation of resources for public facilities has been directed to regional, communal urban centres. The gap between urban and non-urban areas thus persists. One-half of the Slovenian population lives outside such urban centres, only 8–10 per cent are farmers.

Additionally, lower social groups[8] need to live in non-urban areas, commuting to work in industry, keeping farming as an afternoon job. Higher groups more frequently live in urban centres with higher social standards. Nevertheless, there is no traditional connection between poverty and rural life. Those members of high social groups who do live in the countryside, have a high standard of living as well, while some members of lower groups, living in the cities, demonstrate a low urban standard.

Two factors are overlapping here. Those of 'new' social stratification interfere with some of the traditional differences. Some higher social groups thus tend to accumulate privileges within the domain of the allocation of resources for social services and infrastructure. In other words, higher social groups reveal either mobility towards better-built environments, or they demonstrate the power to improve the level of social services in the places where they live. Lower social groups demonstrate less mobility and a lack of social and political power.[9] Some areas thus represent a social trap for those who cannot leave the place or acquire the standard of living to which they contribute their share of income. The result is social and regional segregation, as well as the political deprivation of the lower social groups.

Counter to the aims of social policy, manipulation enables the accumulation of privileges for the 'new class'. Others are left to informal, family resources and the grey economy (residual model, Titmuss 1973). Managing such collective funds, which constitute a substantial share of social financial resources, and making decisions for their distribution, have become a major means of gaining power and privileges, and forming different kinds of social strata which are 'more equal' than others. In Titmuss' (1973) terms it represents 'negative control over resources'.

Political power (CP) has been used for providing 'chosen' loyal people with better access to common goods (especially jobs, social housing of quality, loans, better health services, infrastructure and recreational facilities), enabling a 'red bourgeoisie' to emerge. It mainly consists of top party leaders, socio-political functionaries, top administrators and professional staff in federal or regional institutions, leading managers in the economy, mass media, public services, army, police, etc. Estimates for different kinds of privileges indicate 2–5 per cent of the population as 'a top élite' and 10–20 per cent of those, who are privileged (*QL*, 1988/9, Svetlik, Boh, Tomc, Mandič, Verlič).

What are the results of such a policy?

As a result of the belief (CP) that everything should be changed radically, all humanitarian organisations have been abolished (especially the religious). It was believed that new forms of social policy would be more effective in spite of severe problems of malfunctioning and restrictions present in the early 1960s. However, the concept of 'nestled' social policy was not changed because it symbolised 'good socialist goals' and the values of the new society.

The idea of social policy itself was put in doubt because with the progress of socialism the problems were supposed to disappear (Ruzica 1987, pp. 4, 13). That is why no need was seen for independent social policy but instead for its inclusion in the economy.[10] Every economic crisis increased social differences, which each time were resolved with the redistribution of income to cover the losses of industrial firms, by taking out more loans or printing more money. Financial inflation was the result.

Socialist policies of collective contributions and individual subordination directed to such a consecrated goal as building the new socialist state, are basic to the understanding of socialism. They also define the system of social security which relies on the social sector of activities and privileges for those who are devoted 'soldiers of the revolution', willing to work for sacred aims. Rewards for that, rather than for professional abilities or responsible, productive work, are the basis for making personal careers. Most of the social rights (housing, taking out loans, health care) arose from employment where the greater part of the contributions to socialist economy and development are made. The private sector was only recently allowed to join some social services, like health, education, food and housing provision.

Employment status in the state sector is thus an important socialist domain where political ideology, professional work in the economy and social policy overlap. Changing the very basis of that (political loyalty of management, social property, social or civil rights as the basis of social security, rather than employment status), means the disruption of socialist values. It means the party may lose control over 'the holistic, compact system', where no other interests may be given priority, where no alternatives are allowed. The result would be its loss of social power and its monopolist political position.

'Do not have any illusions about frequent organisational reforms—their role is not to change the very logic of the system' (Ružica 1987, pp. 3, 17). Rather, the aim is to redirect human energy from the resolution of the problems into normative recycling of rules and people, just to create the illusion that it will be better.[11]

The preconditions for such a system to work are:

1. Full employment of the active population. Political decisions for the allocation of economic investments is thus essential.
2. Dominance of the socially owned organisations in economy, provision and social services.
3. Mandatory 'collectivisation' of some basic needs with the obligation to make non-refundable contributions from part of the incomes of firms and individuals.
4. Ideological Party control of these sectors by normative regulations and financing and by 'recycling' loyal personnel in important management positions within such organisations.

If these function well, the result is a totalitarian ideological society. If they do not, more violence, control and restrictions are needed in order to prevent the system from breaking down. And more money is needed to sustain it. Both social security and social privileges within the economy thus have the important function of pacifying and 'integrating' people in a socialist system. They are both instruments of social control, fostering the political regulation of social and individual activities. Given the fact that the first two prerequisites above in Yugoslavia never resulted as planned, there is increasing opposition to the third. What remains for the government is to foster the last one as long as the economy and people can bear it.

The problem of unemployment[12] arose in the early 1960s. The traditional solution of emigration was applied as a temporary measure. The frontiers opened for skilled, educated and professionally ambitious individuals as well, provoking a brain-drain. They also opened for new ideas to come in, enabling comparisons to be made.[13] The other solution was to encourage organisations to employ more workers than necessary for the rational organisation of production. This increased administration on the one hand and extended technologically poor, unskilled production on the other. The bureaucratic federal and regional machinery expanded as well.

The effects of poor production, overemployment and the high cost of new investments required more capital, which was found in foreign markets. Inadequate capital and human investment (political decisions, lack of professional analysis) provoked crises, which ended in economic 'reforms' and financial devaluation.

As a result more compromises to the private and informal (grey economy) sector had to be tolerated in order to prevent social claims expanding. For example, in spite of enormous investment in 'socially built' housing and collective farming, production decreased, the flats and food were (and are) expensive and inadequate according to needs and quality. In 1989/90 the prices for food were higher than in most European countries. The private sector—which offered one of the few possibilities for personal investments—demonstrated high growth, forming today the major share of farming and housing properties.

The 'black market' for some medical services increased, either as illegal private business or as 'extra payment' inside the hospitals. Private services for child-care, cleaning, etc. became a source of income for elderly or unemployed young people. Lately, other private activities have expanded in tourism, services and production for industry, and the provision of food and leisure facilities.

The 'grey economy', afternoon jobs, expanding private sectors of activities and family support are enabling a large part of social sector workers to meet their needs at present. The extent of the grey economy is of such importance that it is a serious obstacle to changing working hours (now from 6 or 7 a.m. to 2 or 3 p.m.) to a European schedule. Economists have estimated (Institute for Economy, 'Delo', 9.7.1988) that 20 per cent of the employed are involved in the 'grey economy'. From 1961 to 1981 the grey economy increased faster than national production, and in 1981 it represented 25 per cent of GNP. Some estimates go up to 40 per cent at present. Estimates of profits in some private sectors total 10 per cent per month and more (Danas July 1990, Zagreb). There is reason to believe that grey and private production have increased even more lately. Only in 1989/90, in Croatia and Slovenia, 30,000 private food stores or other services have been opened. Such activities prevent social conflicts from breaking out, thus performing the role of a social buffer.[14] In small steps, they restructure the economy.

In spite of all the malfunctioning, the high social security of the employed population remains one of the first privileges of the socialist state. This has consequences for the economy which have provoked the political crises. Until the 'ideological obstacles', such as monopoly of the social property or social security within employment, are broken down, little change is to be expected.

Conclusions

Social policy in Yugoslavia paradoxically has enabled a great deal of traditional social differences to persist and has created new ones. First, some regional and urban inequalities of social standard still exist, creating unequal life opportunities for the next generation. This is more evident in the east and south of Yugoslavia than in Slovenia or Croatia.

Second, the proportion of the population that cannot find employment or adequate professional opportunities is increasing. There is no social security for them. This greatly affects the young, skilled generation. Such 'ghettoisation' increases the number of those who are neither entitled to use any existing form of social security nor are able to leave. They depend upon their families. Emigration opportunities are shrinking as well.

Furthermore, employed workers are now losing their jobs and receiving only temporary minimum wages. These do not cover the cost of a minimum standard of living. The proportion of people depending upon the 'grey economy', informal or family resources or on possibilities for emigration is increasing. Without a free labour market the economic and political distinctions between the employed and the unemployed are growing. Normative and ideological restrictions are suffocating any new initiatives.

Social security as one of the fundamental legitimations of socialism has become a pure fiction. It is threatened not only by poor productivity, ineffective social services or counter-productive effects of the 'ideological' social policy, but also threatened by the fact it does not exist for an increasing share of the population.

Without an efficient, active and independent state social policy, we are facing increasing moral and functional problems in socialism. The lack prevents economic restructuring and peaceful political change. It creates a social explosion of riots, poverty and helplessness, thus provoking the use of force and political oppression.

Notes

1. The new 'socialist economy' is used in other categories, but in classical economy it has been invented:
   —Social property is most ambiguous: it belongs to all workers; nobody is 'responsible' for it.
   —We do not produce profit, but income; we do not recognise extra profit or rent.
   —There are varieties of taxes (called contributions) to be paid from total income of each productive organisation, as well as from personal incomes (presently around 56 per cent of gross personal income is paid for public services), which makes the whole system vague and lacking in clarity.
   —Wages are included in a firm's income—surprisingly they do not form part of the production cost, so the large share of contributions diminishes wages.
2. Sub-standard housing has been defined according to space per person, facilities (water supply, bathroom, heating, lighting, etc.) and household equipment.
3. Restructuring is thus a problem: the unemployed can do hardly anything

about it; the overemployed have little or no work assigned; most workers are strategically placed inside the misplaced sector or job; many workers do not have enough raw materials; some factories cannot sell their products; the social sector has gained a monopolist position, which one would not like to lose, etc.

4. A socialist state assures the development of socialism, fraternity and equality among people of different nationalities, promotes the leading role of the Communist party, which is the 'avant-garde' of the labour class and thus represents their interests, as well as 'social interests'.

5. The socialist experience has no interest for social analysis *per se*, since there is now little left of it in Eastern Europe; rather, it makes it an interesting experiment which failed and hopefully is not going to be repeated. Analysis of 'mistakes' is the relevant, priceless human experience in the sense indicated in C. Bosk's book, *Forgive and Remember*, 1979.

6. This included the nationalisation of land, urban properties and productive goods first. Second came the introduction of 'social' property and then, according to merits (veterans of War, CP membership) social rights were distributed. Due to scarce resources, it was called 'redistribution of poverty'. It meant privileges for those at the top of the Party (workers' 'avant-garde') and personnel needed to execute (or control) decisions.

7. *Quality of Life* research embraced data on the national sample of Slovenia (1984–6) and of Yugoslavia (1987–9); it included data for sixteen different nearby facilities available to the inhabitants. Data are presented in one composite indicator with five values, permitting evaluation of the level of services present in different regions to different social groups.

8. Members of lower, middle and higher social groups have been defined (*QL*) according to their position in the working organisation (with management leading), education, political power, profession.

9. It does not necessarily include poverty. Some private farmers and craftsmen, and workers employed in European countries, might become wealthy or acquire prosperous enterprises.

10. In a way, that also ties the worker to the organisation. In systems where no other alternatives exist—such as emigration or the private sector—it was an indirect way to introduce 'forced labour'.

11. Such actions have a special name: 'differentiation'. It means that all those who do not agree with the 'present political line' (CP), have to leave their function or job. The largest of these actions occurred in Croatia and Slovenia during 1971–4 against 'nationalism', where most properous intellectuals have been the victims, together with 'liberal' political leaders and managers.

12. Full employment means an adequate job for an indefinite time in the active life cycle. Self-employment was restricted up to the 1970s to farmers and craftsmen.

13. It is not by chance that most of the real socialist countries severely control their frontiers, exchange of ideas, people's 'opinions' (which can be a criminal offence: Article cod.133) and lifestyle.

14. Findings confirmed in the *Quality of Life* research reports on informal work (I.Svetlik), family and child-care (K. Boh), access to housing provision (S. Mandič), and services in built-up areas (B. Verlič-Dekleva).

Bibliography

Friedmann, Robert R., Gilbert, Neil, Moshe, Sherer, 1987. *Modern Welfare States: a comparative view of trends and prospects*, Sussex.

Hadley, R. and Hatch, S., 1981. *Social Welfare and Failure of the State*, Allen & Unwin, London.

Informativni Bilten, 1987; Review for planning, no. 8–9, dedicated to research into the Restructuring of Social Activities, conducted by authors M. Hanžek, Z. Kolarič, I. Svetlik, J. Šmidovnik at Slovenian Republican Committee for Social Planning and Institute for Sociology, Ljubljana.

Public Opinion Research, 1987/8. Faculty for Sociology, Political Sciences and Journalism, 'Actual themes', 46:18, Ljubljana.

Quality of Life, 1984–9. Research reports from Institute of Sociology, conducted by authors V. Rus, K. Boh (co-ordinators), I. Svetlik, V. Antončič, N. Černigoj Sadar, S. Mandič, M. Pešec, N. Stropnik, G. Tomc, B. Verlič-Dekleva, et al., Lujubljana.

Rein, M. and Morris P., 1982. *Dilemmas of Social Reform*, University of Chicago Press, Chicago.

Ružica, Miroslav, 1985. *Social Policy—criticism of theoretical basis*, School for Social Workers, Belgrade.

——, 1987. *System of Social Policy in Yugoslavia: development and open questions*, report for research project Restructuring of Social Activities, SRC for Social Planning and IS, Ljubljana.

Statistical official reports: *Statistic Year Book* 1987–8 (p. 106) and *Report* 1989 (XXXIII), Federal Institute of Statistics, Belgrade.

Year Book of Health and Social Care in Slovenia, 1988; *Community for Child Care in Slovenia*, 1989, Ljubljana.

Titmuss, M. Richard, 1973. *Social Policy*, Allen & Unwin, London.

Verlič, B. Dekleva, 1986. 'Regional dimensions of the quality of life in Slovenia, *Sociologic overview*, no. 3/4, Zagreb.

——, 1987. 'Theoretical basis for social development of space', *Journal for Critique of Science*, no. 103–4, Ljubljana.

——, 1988. 'Effects of social policy to social structure', *Teorija in praksa*, no. 7–8, Ljubljana.

Woodsworth, David E., 1977. *Social Security and National Policy—Sweden, Yugoslavia, Japan*, McGill-Queen's University Press, Montreal and London.

8 SOCIAL CONSEQUENCES OF HOUSING PROVISION: PROBLEMS AND PERSPECTIVES

Pavel Gantar, Srna Mandič

Any attempt to write on housing provision and its social consequences in Yugoslavia should begin with a caution. The great social, cultural and economic variety of contemporary Yugoslav society prevents us from discussing housing problems in a uniform way. As an example, we consider existing urban—rural differences in Yugoslavia. In backward rural areas which remained largely untouched by socialist urbanisation and industrialisation policies, the single or multi-family house is the predominant culturally acceptable type of dwelling. In such environments where social life is still based on traditional values and various forms of patriarchalism, the large family house[1] represents the values of such a traditional way of life. There is no point investigating why other types of housing provision other than private owned houses are virtually absent

The main aim of this chapter is to show how the idea of housing equality, which is inscribed in the very core of socialist ideology and its developmental policy, turned itself into a contradiction, and instead of creating more equality, it actually brought about new and even more striking inequalities, particularly for certain social strata. Thus the 'story of housing' in socialist societies does not only provide an insight into the peculiarities of housing provision in socialism, but it also illustrates some very important features of socialist development in general.

This chapter on housing provision in Yugoslavia is divided in two parts. In the first part we shall try to look at housing provision within the context of urbanisation and development in Yugoslavia. It is virtually impossible to explain the peculiarities of 'socialist' housing provision in Yugoslavia without paying attention to the role of housing within post-war socialist developmental concepts. However, we shall be able to grasp only the most common features of such development without entering into a detailed explanation of the present Yugoslav variety. The second part of the chapter is devoted to a closer examination of social inequalities in existing modes of housing provision in Yugoslavia.

However, before we approach the subject, it is worthwhile outlining some particular characteristics of housing provision under socialism which are said to be different from those in capitalist market societies. Housing provision (i.e. the production, distribution, use, management and maintenance of housing stock) is based on the following common assumptions:

1. Housing provision is closely linked with the idea of social equality. The link between housing provision and social equality derives from early Marxist and radical critique of market (capitalist) societies. The inequalities in housing provision were regarded as one of the most important social consequences of an 'unjust' social order. It is important to realise that the idea of housing equality, which is meant to replace existing social inequalities, is a very important element in the ideological and political constitution of socialist societies. This is regardless of, as we will see later, the ambiguous meaning of social equality.

2. Housing provision under socialism became associated with the aspirations for the comprehensive and radical reshaping of the everyday social world. This was to be based on solidarity, mutual help and a high level of socialisation and collectivisation of 'household functions' such as child-care, education and some household amenities, i.e. collective laundries etc. The idea was that the new social order should not restrict itself only to the profound transformation of the 'relations of production', but it should also encompass the totality of social life, including the sphere of collective consumption. The spheres of work and collective consumption were to become reintegrated in a sort of new community where the factory and the home were to be closely interwoven. Show-cases of such housing estates based on high levels of collectivisation were built in almost every town where socialist industrialisation took place.[2] Though all such attempts sooner or later failed in fulfilling socialist concepts of a 'new and decent life' for workers, it should be stressed that in socialist states, housing never was 'just' the provision of dwellings for those who need them. It was connected with the idea of a comprehensive transformation of social life and consequently with the struggle for a 'new man' which would correspond to a new social reality. Such ideology in its overt form was present in Yugoslavia until the mid-1960s.

3. Consequently, housing was perceived as a public good that is provided, distributed and maintained by public authorities at the central or local level. This has the following important consequences for housing provision:
   (a) Financial funds for investments in housing construction are collected

through taxation of all the employed population, regardless of housing status.

(b) The costs of housing are not included in the costs of the work-force, for it is assumed that housing provision is a matter of the enterprise or public authorities.

(c) Rents for social rented dwellings do not cover the cost of construction and maintenance of dwellings even in the long term. The result is the deterioration of the housing stock.

4. Another important feature of housing provision is the close relationship between big socially owned construction firms and local and state authorities. The result is a 'territorial division' of construction work among big construction firms and thus their monopolistic position which affects the price of housing construction. Monopolistic position is associated with the tendency to build large housing estates which are most suitable to deploy 'large-scale' construction technology, though the efficiency which is reflected in the prices of housing construction is very low.

During the past forty-five years of socialist development in Yugoslavia the policy of housing provision has changed substantially. Nevertheless, the common assumptions listed above remained unchanged until recently. The results of such ideology of 'socialist housing provision" are the existence of an absolute housing shortage, low quality of state constructed housing stock and high prices of dwellings.

Probably the most striking feature of housing provision in Yugoslavia is the discrepancy between institutional, i.e. formal housing provision, and informal, i.e. self-help housing provision. The institutional system of housing provision cannot satisfy the housing needs of the population. Many people have to rely on their own efforts to obtain a dwelling. There are two main forms of informal housing provision; legal and illegal.[3] Legal but informal self-help construction of one-family houses implies that the 'investors' obtain all the necessary documents for construction. Nevertheless, the house is constructed by a large share of 'non-monetary' means, i.e. the investor's and his/her family's own work, with the help of friends and parents. It usually takes from three to five years to complete the construction and such enterprise is connected with great sacrifices in family life, leisure time, education, etc.

Illegal and informal housing construction is certainly one of the major urban problems in all the largest cities in Yugoslavia. It is carried on without any legal prescriptions and frequently on building-plots that have been assigned to one-family houses. Illegal settlements on the outskirts of the cities are without any communal infrastructure, i.e. without sewerage, water supply and electricity, thus presenting a constant danger to health in the cities. The houses and barracks are in bad condition, and they are constructed mostly of poor quality materials. They provide only elementary housing space. The legal actions against illegally constructed houses are in most cases unsuccessful. The people have to live somewhere. If there are no dwellings to rehouse the families living in illegally constructed houses, extreme actions such as abolishing the illegally constructed houses and barracks are not efficient.

Therefore one can conclude that the 'unintended consequence' of socialist housing provision is that large segments of the population are left to their own skills and abilities to provide more or less 'decent' dwellings for themselves.

Socialist urbanisation and the housing question

Primacy of industrialisation over urbanisation implies that industrialisation (i.e. growth of productive capacities in industry and transition from domestic employment to employment in industry) should proceed much faster than and at the expense of the development of the means of collective consumption, particularly of urban infrastructure. Socialist societies, including Yugoslavia, were based on a specific developmental concept that included extensive industrialisation and transformation of large sections of the population into an industrial working class. Yet, such development was possible only with high rates of industrial growth. Therefore as much as possible of total investment was directed into industry. Investments in the means of collective consumption including housing were postponed until 'better times'. The result was that housing provision could not follow the large transformation of the population into a working class and the migration from rural areas to urban centers.

Systematically encouraged politics of forced industrialisation was possible only at the expense of a cheap labour force and under the assumption that the means of collective consumption are 'free to consume' and therefore they do not enter into the costs of the labour force. Thus the circle which led to the systematic crisis of housing provision was closed. Housing was meant to be the responsibility of the state or local communities, yet because of the 'accumulation problems' of socialist industrialisation, investment in the means of collective production was not a priority. As a result, large sections of the newly urbanised 'working class' were left to solve their housing problems themselves.

Social inequalities and housing provision

The idea of equality has been very important for the Yugoslav socialist project as it provided a source of legitimacy of the system and its future development. Equality, for instance, has helped to legitimise some of the disadvantages socialism has displayed in comparison with the West. Goods, though of lesser quantity than under capitalism, were claimed to be more equally distributed here. Equality was also connected with the future of socialism. It was believed that somewhere along the path towards communism, inequalities, at least those that were unjustified, were bound to fade away. It was in the name of equality that the first revolutionary housing policy was adopted, namely 'the expropriation of the surplus housing floor space',[4] alleviating the inequalities of the past. Indeed, notions of equality have been inherent in the very project of socialism and were the core of its popular support.

Notions of equality in Yugoslav housing

What was the meaning of equality in general and in housing in particular? Was there to be an equality of opportunities or equality of outcomes? Equality according to needs or according to merits? Or should equality be guaranteed only to a minimal level and by whom? In a society where equality is emphasised so much, one should certainly expect to find explicit answers, but this has not been the case in Yugoslavia. Particularly in housing the principle of equality has been only loosely defined and remained open to different meanings and notions. It seems that popular conceptions of equality came to differ substantially from those which were actually institutionalised in housing policy and its norms. It should also be pointed out that in popular notions equality in housing usually referred to allocation of social rental housing. This type of tenure has been, what is sometimes difficult to understand for Western observers, the preferred type of housing by the majority of the urban population.[5]

According to widespread popular notions equality usually signified equal needs (i.e. 'people have equal stomachs and their needs are thus equal'). These completely egalitarian notions were supported by the most abstract constitutional articulation of equal rights, such as the universal right of individuals to social housing, which was, until recently, granted by the Constitution. Yet the subsequent legal acts of housing policy seemed to have institutionalised quite a different and a much more complicated notion of equality, in which criteria of needs were combined with criteria of 'merit'. While a disproportionately large share of publicity was devoted to allocation according to needs—for instance, 'the solidarity rental housing' for marginalised groups—hardly any public attention was devoted to the luxurious rental villas that were allocated according to 'merit'. On a few occasions the reverse was the case and the luxurious housing of members of the top political circles attracted publicity leading to scandals and mass indignation. Yet very frequently the subsequent investigations proved that such housing had been acquired completely legally.[6] This revealed a substantial discrepancy between the legal and the legitimate in the allocation of housing resources—between what is not contrary to the law on the one hand, and to popular notions of social justice on the other hand.

Social outcomes of allocation of housing resources

What was the total outcome of allocation of rental housing with both criteria combined? This has been an important question because the total outcome was neither observed nor discussed by housing policy officials. It was left to Yugoslav urban sociology to analyse, and given the lack of systematic data this was not an easy task. A number of Yugoslav researchers have found the upper strata to be overrepresented in social housing in many towns and regions.[7]

Their general conclusions were very similar to those which Szelenyi (1983) identified under state socialism, which means the following. In conditions of permanent shortage of rental housing, this is the preferred type of tenure by most of the population, and it is declared to be a right, not a market commodity. It is allocated according to the principles of need and merit, favouring the higher social strata. Poorer groups pay more in terms of money and labour because frequently they have to build their own homes. Allocation of privileges and costs through the housing economy has generated not only housing inequalities between different strata, i.e. creating different housing opportunities, but also increased effective income inequalities.

However, this general pattern of housing inequalities under socialism may vary in time and in different social milieux as well as the factors that generate it. One of the fundamental questions, however, is how to explain it. What is the relative weight of 'the state' and 'the market' as its generators? Or is it the result of concepts of equality applied in circumstances of scarcity? Since we are not dealing here with general questions, let us only point out that a very interesting debate is going on about it, with a leading role of Hungarian researchers (Szelenyi 1987; Tosics 1988; Hegedus 1988).

Yugoslav generators of inequalities in housing

As far as housing inequalities in Yugoslavia are concerned, let us point out some particular generators connected to specific institutional arrangements in the Yugoslav system of housing policy. Unlike state socialism, in Yugoslavia the state has made a relatively early and profound retreat from housing provision. Responsibility for provision of rental housing in the mid-1960s shifted to enterprises, and in the mid-1970s also to SHCs (self-managing housing communities) (see details in Mandič, forthcoming). How did each of these two mechanisms generate inequalities in housing opportunities?

First, let us examine enterprise rental housing. By the mid-1960s, rental housing in Yugoslavia became in principle a form of employment benefit. Rental housing was to be allocated by employers (be they a governmental agency, political organisation or an enterprise) to their employees.[8] As was previously pointed out, there was a permanent shortage of this kind of rental provision, which has led to very strong competition between those who could qualify for it according to criteria combining principles both of need (i.e. the present unsatisfactory housing conditions) and merit (i.e. years of employment and position in the employment or political hierarchy). Which principle has prevailed in general? The official data indicate that the allocation of rental housing through this mechanism was biased in favor of 'merits' and not 'needs'. Those with lesser skills were underrepresented among recipients of enterprise rental housing. In 1983 in the Republic of Slovenia, the semi-skilled and the unskilled workers represented 35 per cent of the total employed population. They received only 26.5 per cent of the total of rental dwellings which were allocated in that year. The numbers for the white collar workers were 28 per cent and 37 per cent respectively (Zavod za statistiko SRS 1984).

Besides the competition for housing between the employees inside an institution, an external arena of competition has also emerged. This is where people compete for employment providing more housing benefits. For instance, those employed in governmental self-management and political organisations disposing of a large rental housing stock have a better chance of entering the social rental sector. This may be illustrated by the fact that the group represented 4.1 per cent of the total employed population yet obtained 8.3 per cent of total rental dwellings (JIUS 1987, p. 20). Compared to this, the chances of those with jobs in low-profit labour-intensive industries were much smaller.

Second, let us examine solidarity housing. This programme was established in the mid-1970s. It was to provide rental housing to the groups that were otherwise in a disadvantageous position, i.e. people with very low incomes, young families, retired persons, those employed in low-profit enterprises, etc. Although targeted to special groups, it can hardly be claimed that the programme has improved their housing opportunities, for it has reached only a very small proportion of the population—1 per cent on the national level (Mandič 1988).

Enterprise and solidarity rental housing together, constituting what in Yugoslavia is called 'social housing', amounts to only 20 per cent of the total housing stock and 35 per cent in urban settlements (Savezni zavod za statistiku, 1984). Yet it has been presented as paradigmatic for the self-management based housing policy in Yugoslavia.

How was the rest of the population housed? According to the Population Census in 1981, 70 per cent of the Yugoslav housing stock is owner-occupied, 20 per cent social rental, 5.4 per cent private rental and 4.5 per cent other. To understand the social circumstances of access to homeownership in Yugoslavia, it should be pointed out that purchase is only a minor mode while the dominant mode is self-help construction.[9] Here it should also be pointed out that in the access to non-commercial housing loans, provided by employers and SHCs for buying or building a home, almost identical patterns of inequalities may be found. As in the case of the allocation of rental housing, the upper strata have better access to housing loans.[10] Given the fact that the interest rates on the non-commercial housing loans have not adapted to the high and ever-growing inflation rate, housing loans have provided a rather important mechanism for a part of the upper strata to benefit from inflation. This is so especially where the loan was used to acquire a second home while the first rental was still retained.

Yet another generator of housing inequality has been the personal wealth and earnings of the population. These include not only the formal, registered and taxed earnings but also the informal and unregistered incomes from occupations inside the 'grey economy'. Unlike some other socialist countries, for instance the Soviet Union and Bulgaria, access to personal[11] homeownership was hardly ever subject to administrative restrictions. The individual purchasing power in the market of housing commodities has been perceived in Yugoslavia—within certain limits—as an acceptable source of inequality. The market-generated housing inequalities were never really interfering with popular notions of social justice in housing allocation as was the case in allocation of rental housing.

Recently a new and profound generator of inequalities has emerged. As at the beginning of the 1980s—due to a general economic recession and severe curtailment of investment in housing—conditions of entry into the rental as well as the owner-occupied sectors has substantially worsened. Housing opportunities are becoming increasingly intergenerationally biased. While the already-housed part of the population has retained many past bonuses (deeply subsidised rents and housing loans), the younger cohorts of urban-dwellers are victimised by the lack of available and/or affordable housing options.

Conclusions

Broader social inequalities in terms of income and power have, as we have seen, been reflected also in housing inequalities in Yugoslavia. This is so not only in housing conditions (basic amenities and relative floor space), but also in different housing opportunities and above all in differential access to rental housing and non-commercial housing loans. Moreover, unequal access to these housing resources has led not only to housing inequalities, but also to further inequalities in housing costs and subsequently in real income. Here we come to a very important function that housing has performed in Yugoslavia, where the only legitimate source of inequality was income from 'one's own work'. In circumstances where regular earnings were subject to control and restrictions (the difference between the highest and the lowest incomes inside an enterprise was considered acceptable only within a certain range), the allocation of housing benefits has served as a parallel, mostly hidden vehicle of improving the real income of the upper strata. As for the employees in government agencies and political organisations, housing benefits also served to ensure further their loyalty to the system. In the social turmoil that Yugoslavia witnessed in 1989 and 1990, when the old regime was increasingly losing its credibility and legitimacy, it was the housing of members of the old political élite which has been frequently perceived by the public as the very embodiment of the injustices of the system.

Notes

1. In some regions under the strong influence of Islamic cultural values, families consist of fifteen and even more members living together in one house.
2. Neighbourhood unit built for the workers of the factory 'Litostroj' provides an excellent example. Yet it was never realised as it had been designed (Mihelic 1983, p. 53).
3. For a more detailed account of illegal housing construction, see Kos 1988.
4. Expropriation of the surplus housing was the only concrete suggestion Marx and Engels have ever made about the improvement of workers' housing conditions. It has still to be seen how the 'housing surplus' was defined in Yugoslavia after the Second World War, but it is very likely that the definition did not substantially differ from that which was stated in Lenin's decree in the post-revolutionary Soviet Union, starting from one room per person (Andrusz 1984)
5. As in other socialist countries there are quite a few advantages of the rental housing over the other dominant form of access to housing—building one's own house. Renting is less costly in terms of money (average rent amounts to approximately 4 per cent of the household's income) and effort. Besides, a life-long security of tenure is guaranteed, and also its transfer to one's heirs.
6. An example is the scandal of the villa of Admiral Branko Mamula in 1988.
7. To mention some of them: Živković (1968) in Sarajevo; Čaldarović (1975) and Seferagić (1977) in Zagreb; Petovar and Janković (1980) and Vujović (1986) in Belgrade.
8. Terms like 'employers' and 'employees' are used here only to avoid misunderstanding. However, in the Yugoslav system the relationship between the 'employers' and the 'employees' should be understood in terms of self-management, meaning that the elected representatives of 'employees' participate

in 'employers' functions. The following are the particular functions concerning housing: to determine how much of the enterprise's income should be devoted to the housing needs of the employees; to decide how much of it should be used to produce housing for rent and/or housing loans for the employees (to purchase, renovate or construct their own homes); to operate the criteria of allocation of both rental housing and loans.

9. *Qualify of Life* in Yugoslavia survey shows the following relative proportions of different types of access to housing by the adult population: 26 per cent of the population have acquired their housing unit by means of self-help construction, 6 per cent by purchase, 15 per cent by means of inheritance, 28 per cent by inhabiting a unit that is owned by a relative other than a spouse, 18 per cent by renting social housing and 4 per cent by renting private housing (Mandič 1988, p. 23).

10. According to *Quality of Life* in Slovenia, in the group of those who have built their own homes, only 2 per cent of the higher strata did not receive any loans, compared with 44 per cent in the lowest strata (Mandič 1986, p. 201).

11. In most socialist countries there is a distinction between personal and private ownership. Personal ownership over a commodity is related to personal use of the commodity.

References

Andrusz, G., 1984. *Housing and Urban Development in the USSR*, Macmillan, London.

Čaldarović, O., 1975. 'Neki pokazatelji prostorne socijalne diferenciacije i socijalne segregacije stanovništva Zagreba' (Some indicators of spatial social differentiation and social segregation in Zagreb), *Revija za sociologiju 1975/4*.

Hegedus, J., 1988. 'Inequalities in East European cities: a reply to Ivan Szelenyi', *International Journal of Urban and Regional Research*, vol. 11, no. 1, pp. 129–32.

Kos, Drago, 1988. 'Neformalne dejavnosti in prostorski razvoj' (Non-formal activities and spatial development), in Svetlik et al., *Neformalno delo*, Delavska enotnost, Ljubljana.

Jugoslovenski Institut za Urbanizam i Stanovanje, 1987. *Stambena politika i stanovanje u SFRJ* (Housing politics in Yugoslavia), JIUS, Belgrade.

Mandič, S., 1986. 'Obezbeaivanje stana kao organičenog dobra'. (A provision of housing as a goods in scarce supply), *Socioloski pregled*, vol. 20, no. 3–4, pp. 195–206.

—— 1988. 'Prispevek k opisu stanovanjske preskrbe v Jugoslaviji'. (A contribution to the description of housing provision in Yugoslavia), Research Report, ISU, Ljubljana.

—— forthcoming. 'Housing provision in Yugoslavia: changing roles of the state, market and informal sectors', in Willem van Vliet and Jan van Weesep (eds), *The Changing Role of Government in Housing: studies of privatization and decentralization in seven countries*, Sage.

Mihelič, B., 1983. *Urbanistični razvoj Ljubljane* (Urban development of Ljubljana), Partizanska knjiga, Ljubljana.

Petovar, K., i Janković, I., 1980. 'Rezidencijalna segregacija' (Residental segregation), *Dometi*, 80/11.

Svetlik, I. et al., 1988. *Neformalno delo* (Non-formal work), Delavska enotnost, Ljubljana.
Szelenyi, I., 1983. *Inequalities under state socialism*, Oxford University Press, New York.
—— 1987. 'Housing inequalities and occupational segregation in state socialist cities', *International Journal of Urban and Regional Research*, vol. 11, no. 1, pp. 1–8.
Tosics, I., 1988. 'Inequalities in East European cities: can redistribution ever be equalising, and if so, why should we avoid it?: a reply to Ivan Szelenyi', *International Journal of Urban and Regional Research*, vol. 12, no. 1, pp. 133–6.
Vujovič, S., 1986. 'Društvena slojevitost i stanovanje u Beogradu' (Social stratification and the housing in Belgrade), *Sociološki pregled*, vol. 20, no. 3–4, pp. 179–94.
Zavod za statistiko SR Slovenije, 1984. *Statisticni letopis SR Slovenije* (Statistical Annuals of the Socialist Republic of Slovenia), Ljubljana.
Zivkovič, M., 1968. 'Jedan primer segregacije u razvoju naših gradova' (An example of segregation in the development of our cities), *Sociologija*, 3/1968.

Further reading

Andrusz, G., 1984. *Housing and Urban Development in the USSR*, Macmillan, London.
Hegedus, J., 1987. 'Reconsidering the roles of the state and the market in socialist housing systems', *International Journal of Urban and Regional Research*, vol. 11, no. 1, p. 70–97.
Hegedus, J. and Tosics, I., forthcoming. 'Filtration and innovation in Hungarian housing', in Willem van Vliet and Jan van Weesep (eds), *The Changing Role of Government in Housing*, Sage.
Konrad, G. and Szelenyi, I., 1977. 'Social conflicts of Underurbanisation', in Michael Harloe (ed.), *Captive Cities. Studies in the Political Economy of Cities and Regions*. John Wiley & Sons, Chichester.
Szelenyi, I., 1981. 'The relative autonomy of the state or state mode of production', in Michel Dear and Allen J. Scott (eds), *Urbanisation & Urban Planning in Capitalist Society*, Methuen, London and New York.
—— 1989. 'Housing policy and the emergent socialist mixed economy of Eastern Europe', *Housing Studies*, vol. 4, no. 3, pp. 167–76.
—— forthcoming. 'Development in socialist economies', in Willem van Vliet and Jan van Weesep (eds), *The Changing Role of Government in Housing*, Sage.
Tosics, I., 1987. 'Privatization in housing policy: the case of the Western countries and that of Hungary', *International Journal of Urban and Regional Research*, vol. 11, no. 1, pp. 61–78.

9 SOCIALIST URBANISATION AND SOCIAL SEGREGATION

Ognjen Čaldarović

Introduction

In this chapter we shall discuss some of the concepts of 'social justice' and their application to the study of social stratification in urban areas in Yugoslavia. In urban sociology, the concept of 'social justice' is an important illustration of the application of socialism to urban space or to space in general. The main advantage of socialism compared with capitalism is that some 'socialist values' can be distributed properly and equally (for everybody) throughout the space of a concrete society.[1] The precise meaning of the 'distribution' is that within that kind of society surplus value (or profits) could be 'deconcentrated', 'broken down' and then, according to the principles of social justice, distributed equally to everybody. The main problem which confronts the 'distribution' will be who decides and the criteria of distribution. Who decides will be easily resolved—in socialist societies it is the party; and the criteria too—they are the intrinsic values of socialism. The only remaining question will be the efficient distribution of these values.[2]

The functioning of that 'model' could become more interesting if someone tries to discuss the distribution of different social groups, strata or even classes in the inevitably unequal conditions of urban living in a concrete city and society. It will be very close to the truth if we say that equal conditions for everybody in urban living are to be found hardly anywhere. This applies also in socialist societies. Different researches and investigations in many countries have shown that 'quality of (urban) living' is necessarily unequal and that inequality cannot be explained by the 'malfunctioning' of social justice, but rather by the 'work' of some more or less systematic forces behind the simple fact of social differentiation in space. In urban sociology social stratification is usually called social segregation or residential segregation.[3]

Terms

Županov, following Sorokin, explains the notion of social differentiation as a kind of 'horizontal stratification', and social stratification is a system of structured social inequalities.[4] 'Structure' and 'system' mean that social facts are not a product of some unexpected consequences, or a by-product of some 'mistakes' in the distribution of social justice, but rather facts which have their origins and systematic sources. The study of social stratification in a given society can show that a relatively stabilised pattern can exist and that the groups can be divided at least according to the political, economical and professional positions they occupy on the imaginary ladders of social stratification.

The problem of establishing the 'right' picture of social stratification is rather difficult in every society, but we shall mention some which are more or less typical for socialist societies. The approach to the study of social structure in Yugoslav society was, in the last twenty years, more or less systematic a priori research into social structure. It included all the approaches which tried to apply a theoretic model of social structure to the real structure of a given society. The main problem which appeared was that the group called 'the rest' sometimes grew so much that it became a major group formed from all the groups which did not 'fit' into the preconceived ideas of a theoretical typology of social structure of a given society. The typologised approach which was in the past mostly a combination of theoretical and empirical typologies of social structure made some progress in research because it applied different criteria, and the picture of social structure appeared as a multidimensional framework.[5]

The problem of a 'grey zone', which is used by Županov in his work about social stratification,[6] could also be very usefully applied to the study of all of the social problems, especially in socialist societies, which did not 'fit' into the institutionally accepted and approved image of a given society. Social segregation or residential segregation as well as social stratification in a socialist society, is 'pushed' to the margin, or into the 'grey zone'. Županov interestingly applies the concept of 'the function of stratification', which raises the question of the efficiency of socialist societies in general. Before anyone can try to determine 'the function' of social segregation, however, he will have to try 'to push' it out from the 'grey zone' of institutionally unapproved social phenomena. Moreover, the 'functionalisation' of social segregation will probably lead to the complication of social relations in general and will give cause for new social actions. The only advantage of the institutionalisation and functionalisation of social segregation would be that this social fact would be publicly, politically and scientifically discussed and eventually (one day) 'solved'.

The notion of 'egalitarian syndrome' which Županov also discusses in his works, could be of help in a study of residential segregation in Yugoslavia. This notion can be easily explained as a way of predominant public behaviour: if we are to suffer, let us suffer equally. In other words, social groups expect to be distributed on the imaginary ladder of social stratification in such a way that 'suffering' is equally distributed among everybody.

Main approaches to the study of social structure in Yugoslavia

The analysis of different studies of social structure of Yugoslav society will show that we can differentiate several approaches.[7] The integrationist approach insists on the idea of 'friendly classes', as opposed to the conflict approach which insists on discord between classes in Yugoslav society. 'Integrationists' suppose that if we find classes at all in Yugoslav society, they would be 'friendly' or just be the remainder of some old, pre-revolutionary classes which existed in the past. The idea of a classless society is very close to the idea of the integrationists and also not very far from the idea of a one class society. If we are to find classes in Yugoslavia, we shall find only one class, and eventually it will be the working class (in its enlarged variety this approach is known also as a 'working people' approach). If we are all 'working people', then we are all in the same boat. There are not so many differences between us, and of course no stratification, segregation or inequality.

The dichotomy approach was also applied in the past in several ways. The first (mostly in the 1970s) insisted that generally speaking one could find only two basic classes in Yugoslav society—the working class and the 'counterclass'. The working class was not difficult to define. Its members were mostly defined as those workers who worked manually. However, the 'counterclass' was difficult to define except for one thing, its 'normal' and obvious antagonism towards the working class. The 'counterclass' thus became a big conglomerate of everything and everybody who could not fit into the 'manually' defined working class. The second, newer variety of the dichotomy approach insists on many criteria when establishing possible strata and classes, such as social status, social position, party membership, 'lifestyle', quality of living, number of devices and appliances in the home, and so on. At first, researchers were trying to 'push' all the different strata into two clearly established classes, and the rest appeared as a 'middle class' or stratum. Later and newer approaches did not insist on a basic dichotomy but identified several classes or layers or strata.

The investigation of residential segregation in Yugoslavia

Several researches on residential segregation have been done in the last twenty years, mostly in larger towns and cities—Belgrade, Zagreb, Sarajevo, Ljubljana.[8] All the studies found that residential segregation existed and that a pattern could be established. Members of social groups higher on the social ladder would also have a better 'quality of urban life'. At first, researchers combined simple criteria and indicators such as the size of residence, number of people living in a given apartment or house, number of square metres per person, number of persons per room, etc., and lately some other indicators were included such as the proximity of public transport and other facilities, quality of residential location, quality of the immediate environment and its ability to satisfy the basic and 'other' needs of the local population.

The researchers define residential segregation as a social fact emerging not 'by chance', but as one of the results of the general inequality of social groups in society. Some were also using the term homogenisation to define the agglomeration of a population of the same characteristics occupying the same residential area of a given city or town. The opposite was a heterogeneous social structure, which was used as a concept in researches to show a 'good' mixture of different social groups living close to one another in the same residential positions, and so having relatively the same 'quality of urban life'. Homogenisation and heterogenisation are long processes which are based on different developments through time, such as migration patterns, patterns of city growth, the basic characteristics of migratory populations, basic characteristics of urban planning and policy, the basic features of housing policy, etc.

The fundamental assumption of almost any investigation of residential segregation in Yugoslavia was that in general the established social structure of a given city should be found to be more or less the same in each of its residential parts (communes, municipalities or districts). A 'balanced' social structure was one with balanced social groups in residential areas of a given city. An 'unbalanced' social structure was used to denote a segregated population.

That idealistic idea of repetition of a given social structure of society in its smaller parts was very difficult to find in Yugoslavia as in every other society. In the societies in which the 'egalitarian syndrome' determines very strongly public behaviour, it is not normal to expect the better-off people to segregate themselves and settle in the best residential areas. The same goes for those who are down the ladder. Everybody has to have more or less the same quality of urban life. If we find social segregation, it means that some 'mistakes' were made in the past which can be repaired in the future.[9]

That 'reparation' is obviously not happening, and differences in the quality of urban life are widening. The distribution of housing rights can also show which social groups have these rights, and which groups do not. According to the results of an investigation of social structure in Croatia carried out by the Institute for Social Research and Department of Sociology of the University of Zagreb between 1984 and 1986, 16 per cent of workers are in possession of housing rights, 25 per cent of clerks, 37 per cent of the intelligentsia, 54 per cent of general managers (directors) and 57 per cent of politicians. This shows that different social groups have different social positions in the 'distribution'. A complementary set of statistics is also of interest. Out of all the housing production in Yugoslavia, around 60–80 per cent is produced as family housing, meaning that people build houses using their own resources, relatives, friends, etc. That type of housing practice is exercised mostly by workers because they are left with only that solution.

Home ownership can also show us some differences. It is understandable that houses are owned by workers mostly, and politicians the least (47 per cent and 29 per cent, respectively). The distribution of housing rights is only one of the indicators of social segregation in general. Table 9.1 shows how the different groups are placed in that distribution.[10]

'Equal distribution' of all social groups according to their representation in the distribution of 'housing rights' would be an 'ideal', especially if one takes into account that enterprises are looking mostly for highly educated people and giving to that social group the most advantages in solving their housing problems.

Table 9.2 shows the unequal distribution of different social groups on the 'waiting lists' for housing rights in Croatia in 1986. This data can be accompanied by some other data which show that some social groups in

Table 9.1 Index of participation of some social groups according to the level of education in the distribution of 'housing rights' in Croatia, 1974, 1976 and 1978

	1974	1976	1978
1. University education	2.6	1.9	2.5
2. Highly skilled workers	1.6	1.8	1.2
3. Middle educated	1.3	1.2	1.2
4. Skilled workers	0.8	0.9	0.7
5. Lower educated	0.8	0.6	1.2
6. Semi-skilled workers	0.7	0.6	0.6
7. Unskilled workers	0.4	0.5	0.7

Table 9.2 Distribution of some social groups according to their level of education and the time spent on the 'waiting lists' for housing rights in Croatia in 1986

	Per cent
1. Skilled workers	37.2
2. Unskilled workers	13.2
3. Semiskilled workers	12.2
4. Highly skilled workers	11.4
5. Middle educated professionals	10.9
6. University educated professionals	9.7
7. Low educated professionals	2.9

the distribution of housing rights are systematically underprivileged. The actual housing standard in the country is low: for example, in Belgrade in 1975 the average housing space per person was only 14 square metres, and the range was from 2 to 120 square metres per person.[11] Using the categories developed by Chombart de Lauwe[12] of 'critical' and 'pathological' housing minimum, Zivković finds that in 1975 in Belgrade 226,000 inhabitants were living below the 'pathological' threshold (12–124 square metres per person), and 228,000 were living below the 'critical' threshold (8–10 square metres per person).

Some newer data in Croatia show that in 1985, 50 per cent of workers, 30 per cent of clerks and 25 per cent of the intelligentsia (including many of the university instructors and assistants) had only 15 square metres per person. Housing standards in Yugoslavia are relatively low. The average size of housing space in Croatia has changed just slightly between 1951 and 1971 (from 41.3 to 49.6 square metres), and in cities and towns from 48.3 to 50.3 square metres.[13] This relatively low quality of housing standards will, in the future, raise some questions about the creation of slums, especially in our 'new settlements'.

One example of residential segregation (Zagreb)

Zagreb, as a relatively big town by Yugoslav standards, has almost 1,000,000 inhabitants ('greater Zagreb') and has been growing rapidly since 1960. The social structure of the city has been changing all the time, especially through some mass intervention in the building of new housing units, highly concentrated and built on relatively small plots. We shall have a closer look at the figures of the censuses taken in 1971 and 1981 to see the distribution of social groups in different local communities (municipalities, administrative units) of Zagreb. We shall compare data concerning the level of education, the level of qualification of the employed population, and compare this data with the living conditions.

Municipalities in Zagreb as administrative units are obviously different and house various populations in differing proportions. Nevertheless, it will be found that a stable pattern exists, and that certain social groups found in some municipalities are not found in others. The comparison of two censuses which cover ten years will show that the situation is unchanged (Table 9.3). For our purposes we shall take only four minicipalities, of which the first two will be called 'elite' (Centar, Medveščak), and the other two 'peripheral' (Dubrava, Susedgrad).

Table 9.4 shows data about the distribution of employed inhabitants in some of the municipalities of Zagreb according to their level of qualifications. What kind of conclusions can we draw from this data? It is obvious that

Table 9.3 Social structure of inhabitants of some of the municipalities of Zagreb in 1971 and 1981

Municipalities	University education (%)		Middle educated people (%)		Without education (%)	
	1971	1981	1971	1981	1971	1981
1. CENTAR	27	36	23	29	5	2
2. MEDVEŠČAK	32	37	24	28	4	2
3. DUBRAVA	5	10	11	20	12	5
4. SUSEDGRAD	5	9	12	21	11	4
Total (Zagreb)	16	19	19	25	8	4

Table 9.4 Social structure of employed population according to the level of skill for selected municipalities of Zagreb in 1971 and 1981

Municipalities	Skilled and highly skilled workers (%)		Unskilled and semi-sk. workers (%)	
	1971	1981	1971	1981
1. CENTAR	19	15	11	6
2. MEDVEŠČAK	16	13	8	6
3. DUBRAVA	32	28	28	18
4. SUSEDGRAD	32	29	26	19
Total (Zagreb)	25	23	17	13

the two first municipalities are characterised by one type of social structure, and the other two by another. The differences between the composition of the populations of these four municipalities can be explained also through differences between the 'centre' and the 'periphery'. The central municipalities of Zagreb have better educated populations and the peripheral less educated inhabitants. These differences were constant over ten years, showing only slight changes.

Social segregation of the population is very well established if we point out that in 1981, in the municipality of Centar, there were three times more inhabitants with university education than in the municipality of Dubrava. In the municipality of Medveščak there were four times more inhabitants with a university education than in the municipality of Susedgrad. The pattern of social segregation in Zagreb is relatively simple. The lower strata live on the periphery and the higher strata in the centre of the city. We can also deduce from this pattern that social segregation is demonstrated primarily by the lack of equal representation of the inhabitants with higher education in the peripheral parts of the city, rather than the overrepresentation of some specific strata of the population in the centre. Because in Yugoslavia we can find hardly any kind of clear class or ethnic segregation, a pattern of 'dispersed' segregation has emerged.

If we examine the groups of skilled and unskilled workers in the 'elite' and 'peripheral' municipalities, we can see here, too, some interesting differences. It is clear that the number of all kinds of 'workers' in Zagreb is decreasing. What will be of interest for the discussion of social segregation in one city is that in the 'elite' municipalities we find three times fewer unskilled workers than in the 'peripheral' municipalities.

If we compare the composition of social structure and the conditions of housing (quality of urban life) in some small areas of the municipalities, we shall see that there is a systematic correlation between better and worse housing conditions with higher and lower social strata. Looking, for example, at the social structure of two zones in the 'elite' municipality of Medveščak in Zagreb, we see that in the central zone more than 50 per cent of the inhabitants had a university education, and the average size of apartments was in the range of 55–75 square metres. The situation was quite different in one 'peripheral' zone in the same municipality. There we find more than 60 per cent of the inhabitants with various levels of workers' qualifications, and the average size of the apartments was only 48 square metres.

In another part of the city, one zone, of whose inhabitants 60 per cent were workers, had an average size of housing unit of only 40 square metres, the number of persons per room was 1.67, the average number of households was 1.28 per apartment, and the average number of inhabitants per apartment was 3.27. The average housing space per person was only 12.24 square metres. Comparing that zone with a 'better' zone, we discovered another structure of the population as well as another 'quality of life'. In that zone more than 50 per cent of the population had a university education and their housing conditions were much better. The average size of the apartments was 56.3 square metres, average number of rooms per apartment was 2.11, average number of households per apartment was 1.12, the average number of inhabitants per apartment was 3.17 persons, the average number of inhabitants per room was 1.5 persons, and the average housing space per person was 17.25 square metres.[14]

These data could be accompanied by other data. However, there is no doubt that a relatively stable pattern of social segregation exists in Zagreb. The data we present have more weight because they are drawn from the censuses and therefore have more 'objectivity'. Analysing that data one discovers that social segregation in Zagreb could be explained through mechanisms of systematic homogenisation of population in defined areas of the city. This pattern can be specified. It is characterised by the lack of higher strata in the peripheral parts of the city and not by the overrepresentation of any strata in the central areas. This pattern could be called 'dispersed segregation'.

Conclusion

Social segregation in space is found in many socialist societies.[15] However, in many socialist societies this is still widely neglected and is seen even as a 'normal' fact of life. Nevertheless, the basic idea of egalitarian societies presupposes that every member of society will have (more or less) equal opportunities for pursuing the same 'quality of urban life'. If the idea and reality of social segregation are officially institutionalised and sanctioned, it would mean that ideas of equality, socialism, social justice and egalitarianism would have to be abandoned.[16]

However, failure to recognise social segregation does not mean that it does not exist. It means only (at least in Yugoslav society) that that fact of social life is being pushed constantly into the 'grey zone.' The avoidance of institutional recognition of social segregation leads only to the postponement of taking any measures to change the situation. So, social segregation in Yugoslav society is 'floating around', sometimes being completely neglected, sometimes being discussed only within closed circles.

In conclusion, let us analyse what led to social and residential segregation in Yugoslavia, using the example of one city:

1. Mass migration to the city, mostly oriented to its outskirts. The migrants of the 1960s and 1970s consisted mostly of unskilled and skilled workers. This pattern of migration contributed also to the pattern of residential segregation discussed earlier in this chapter.
2. The construction of mass housing units in the 1960s and 1970s can be

viewed as the concentrated housing of population on relatively small plots. The type of population in 'new settlements' is heterogeneous and the effect on social segregation was 'positive'. Residential segregation is decreasing because the level of heterogeneity of population is increasing.

3. The loss of population from the centre of the city is also relevant to the discussion of social segregation in space. It was not the result of suburbanisation, but rather of many intervening factors such as the death of the older generation, the breaking of the pattern of subletting apartments and the conversion of housing into office space. The emptying of the city centre in the 1960s and 1970s caused the rapid development of slums and the birth of ideas for 'city rehabilitation'. Nevertheless, the first impact of the 'emptying' was a worsening of the social balance at the core of the city.

4. 'City renewal' was also an important development in the 1960s and 1970s and which had a strong impact on the changes in the social composition of the population. The 'city renewal' movement could also be seen as a rehabilitation of the city's social structure by different processes such as construction of housing units in the city centre, which would house 'new' inhabitants, i.e. a new social structure. The general impact on the structure of the city center was positive because it created a 'new' and 'better' social structure of inhabitants and halted the spread of slums. However, the intensity of construction in the city centre was not so great and the changes in the composition of the population were mostly marginal. Nevertheless, in the long run these changes could affect the social composition of the population, increase the level of heterogeneity and thus contribute to the establishment of a more 'balanced' social structure of inhabitants in the central area.

5. We also predict that decreased immigration from the end of the 1970s and from the beginning of the 1980s (because of the growing social and economic crisis in the country) will bring some changes in the social composition of the population, and thereby affect also residential segregation. Reduced immigration to the city can bring a rise in the standard of living, especially in consumption, improvements in the quality of different services such as public transport, the 'quality or urban life' in general as well as the quality of housing on the personal level. All these processes could lead to the equalisation of social segregation in general, to the reduction of social differences to a minimum, and to a rise in the level of heterogeneity. However, no prediction can be taken for granted in the social sciences, especially in a country where housing space is probably among the most expensive in the world.

Notes

1. See especially D. Harvey, *Social Justice and the City*, E. Arnold, London.
2. See, for example, the opinion of M. Castells about the 'advantages' of socialist urbanisation in his book, *The Urban Question—the Marxist approach*, E. Arnold, London.
3. See D. Seferagić, 1977 and O. Čaldarović, 1975.
4. See J. Županov, 1977.
5. See D. Sekulić, 1983.
6. See J. Županov, 1977.
7. See detailed explanation in D. Sekulić, 1983.
8. See details in M. Živković, 1981, D. Seferagić, 1977, O. Čaldarović, 1975, S. Vujović, 1977.
9. In Yugoslavia we cannot speak about ethnic segregation yet, but mostly about segregation on the basis of class, occupation or social status. First signs of possible ethnic segregation are just appearing in the province of Kosovo, in Slovenia and in parts of Croatia, where some ethnic groups are concentrated in certain parts of some cities.
10. See details in G. Bežovan et al., 1987.
11. See details in M. Živković, 1981.
12. P. H. Chombart de Lauwe, *Famille et habitation*, CNRS, Paris, 1959, vols 1 and 2.
13. See G. Bežovan et al., 1987.
14. See details in O. Čaldarović, 1975.
15. See for example J. Musil, 1980; French and Hamilton, 1979, I. Szelenyi, 1981; and some Yugoslav authors.
16. Some 'radical' moves in some of the socialist countries in the recent past had shown all the problems of dealing with the 'revolutionary treatment' of social segregation. Experiments with 'deurbanisation' in Cuba, 'ruralisation' of Havana ruined that city almost completely. Oscillations of urban policy in China in the 1960s and 1970s showed that urban policy could only with great difficulty jump over the level of political and economic development. The most frightening example is the radical 'deurbanisation policy' followed in Phnom Pen in Cambodia by Pol Pot. It seemed (for the time being) that Pol Pot had succeeded in emptying the main city of one country, following somehow the theoretical ideas of deurbanisation policies and of 'equal' distribution of inhabitants throughout the territory. See details in H. Stretton, 1978.

References

Bežovan, Gojko et al., 1987. 'Stambena politika i stambene potrebe' (Housing policy and housing needs), *Radničke novine*, Zagreb.

Castells, Manuel, 1977. *The Urban Question—the Marxist approach*, E. Arnold, London.

Čaldarović, Ognjen, 1975. 'Neki pokazatelji prostorne socijalne diferencijacije i socijalne segregacije stanovništva Zagreba 1971, godine (Some data about spatial

differentiation and segregation of the Zagreb population in 1971), *Revija za sociologiju* (Sociological Review), Zagreb, no. 4, vol. 4, pp. 58–66.
French, R.A. and Hamilton, I., (eds.) 1979, *The Socialist City*, E. Arnold, London.
Harvey, David, 1975. *Social Justice and the City*, E. Arnold, London.
Musil, Jiri, 1980. 'Urbanisation in socialist countries', *International Journal of Sociology*, vol. 10, no. 2–3.
Seferagić, Dušica, 1977. Socijalna segregacija u rezidencijalnom prostoru/primjer Zagreba/(Social Segregation in the Residential Area—The example of Zagreb/), M. A. thesis, Faculty of Philosophy, University of Zagreb.
Sekulić Duško, 1983. 'O pristupima proučavanju stratifikacione strukture jugoslavenskog društva' (Approaches to the study of stratification structure of Yugoslav society), *Sociologija* (Sociology), Belgrade, no. 1, pp. 1–21.
Szelenyi, Ivan, 1981. 'Structural changes and alternative to capitalist development in the contemporary urban and regional systems', *International Journal or Urban and Regional Research*, vol. 5, no. 1, pp. 1–15.
Stretton, Hugh, 1978. *Urban Planning in Rich and Poor Countries*, Oxford University Press, Oxford.
Vujović, Sreten, 1977. 'Problem socijalističkog grada' (A problem of a socialist city), *Kultura* (Culture), no. 39, Belgrade.
Živković, Miroslav, 1981. *Prilog jugoslovenskoj urbanoj sociologiji* (A contribution to the Yugoslav Urban Sociology), Belgrade.
Županov, Josip, 1977. 'Sociologija i samoupravljanje' (Sociology and self-management), *Školska knjiga*, Zagreb.

Further reading

Specific articles on social segregation (residential segregation) in socialist societies in English are rather difficult to find. In the following list will be found a discussion of different aspects of segregation, especially in socialist societies or in the societies which have recently called themselves 'socialist'.

Burns, R. T. et al., 1981. *Citizen Participation in Housing Management and Local Community Development: the case of Yugoslavia*, University of Uppsala, Uppsala.
Čaldarović, Ognjen, 1987. 'Some problems of housing development in Yugoslavia', *Sociological Review of Kobe University*, Kobe University, no. 4, pp. 115–32.
——1983. 'State, economy and legitimacy (paper).
——1987. 'Market socialism' and civil society: the limits of state intervention in Yugoslavia' (paper).
——1988. 'Concept of housing and forms of privatisation in Yugoslavia' (paper).
Konrad, G. and Szelenyi, I., 1977. 'Social conflicts of underurbanisation', in: Harloe, M. (ed), 1977. *Captive Cities*, J. Wiley and Sons, London, pp. 157–74.
Szelenyi, I., 1987. 'Housing inequalities and occupational segregation in state socialist cities', in *International Journal of Urban and Regional Research*, vol. 11, no. 1, pp. 1–9.
Zukin, Sh., 1987. 'Gentrification: culture and capital in the urban core'. *Annual Review of Sociology*, no. 13, pp. 129–47.

PART V
CONCLUSIONS

10 GENERAL LESSONS FROM THE YUGOSLAV EXPERIENCE

James Simmie and Jože Dekleva

Introduction

In this chapter we seek to draw some general conclusions based on the detailed analyses presented, by our mainly Slovenian writers, in the preceding chapters. Our conclusions focus on the theoretical implications of the Yugoslav empirical material; the constraints and limits confronting the Yugoslav socialist experiment in particular and their implications for other East European states in general; and the lessons that may be learnt from the Yugoslav experience for the future redevelopment of the country itself and other countries in Eastern Europe.

In seeking to draw these more general conclusions from our detailed and specific empirical material, we should first point to some of its unique features which should be borne in mind when interpreting this exercise. It is only right to stress that Yugoslavia is both unique in some ways and an illustration of more general East European countries in others.

It is unique in the sense that unlike other East European states, the single-party communist government did have widespread popular support during its early years. This was a result of its role in the liberation struggles against Nazi Germany. Its success in this struggle gave the party a legitimacy not enjoyed in such measure elsewhere. Yugoslavia is also unique because the legitimacy enjoyed by the party made it stronger and more able to tolerate both decentralisation and some dissent. This limited flexibility has also allowed it to adapt piecemeal to developing democratic movements less dramatically than elsewhere in Eastern Europe.

The distinctive innovation of worker self-management was seen, by some other East European states, as an important initiative contributing to the achievement of both Marxist goals and legitimacy. It was accordingly copied in varying degrees by Poland, Hungary and the Union of Soviet Socialist Republics (USSR) during the 1980s. In common with other East

European states, Yugoslavia sought to introduce a variety of Marxist/ Leninist socialism as an alternative to West European capitalist and democratic regimes. In common with other East European countries, however, the communist project has not achieved its stated objectives and has declined politically with its inability to manage the economy to the extent that more people perceive themselves to be worse off than they would be in European market economies.

While there is no way to 'prove' conclusively that a collective economy and self-management cannot work under any circumstances, it has been shown that in the limited possibilities facing Yugoslavia after the Second World War, they have been inadequate for the tasks confronting them. In some respects the possibilities for the success of such a project were greater in the non-aligned Yugoslav case than in other East European states. The fact that by general consent it has failed there may allow the conclusion that it cannot succeed in the long run elsewhere either.

Theoretical conclusions

A major reason for studying East European countries, such as Yugoslavia, is to be able to evaluate Marxist theory in practice and hence the validity of the theory itself. Most of the communist regimes of Eastern Europe, including Yugoslavia, were established on the basis of Marxist theory and its Leninist practice. At the end of the day the experiment appears to have failed. This indicates that there are serious flaws in the original ideas themselves as well as in their practice.

We argue here that three major Marxist concepts are called into question by the empirical experiences of East European states following Marxist/ Leninist practice. They are (1) the significance attributed to the role of private property; (2) the relevance of the conception of a 'classless' society; and (3) the direction of history.

The role of private property in capitalist societies is seen by Marx as one which forms the basis of a set of exploitative social relationships between owners and non-owners. East European experience has shown that the abolition of private productive economic property only serves to introduce different forms of exploitation and extremely inefficient use of such resources. Even in the self-management system of economic decision-making, in Yugoslavia, major decisions and resulting benefits remained in the hands of the political and managerial élites. When workers tried to acquire more of the comparatively rare surpluses generated in their 'own' enterprises, they were eventually prevented from receiving them on the basis of the familiar and 'correct' argument that they were required for essential investments to generate future economic growth.

In fact, the theoretical significance attached by Marxist theorists to the creation of 'surplus' value and capital accumulation imbues a very simple observation with much more explanatory power than it deserves. As most communist regimes have discovered by experience, economies must generate some surpluses and accumulate somewhere or they stagnate and decline. The disadvantages of not generating much surplus is exemplified in Yugoslavia by the fact that the national economy has grown by 30 per cent less than comparable Southern European market economies since the Second World War. Other East European economies have fared even worse.

The second Marxist concept which has also emerged as a more academic than a practical reality is the concept of a classless society. This rested on theoretical connections between the ownership of property and Marx's particular definition of social class. The abolition of private property was axiomatically supposed to produce a classless society. This, however, has not proved to be a particularly significant change either in Yugoslavia, or indeed, elsewhere. The definitional abolition of social classes has by no means removed equally important forms of social stratification in the everyday lives of those living in communist regimes.

Paradoxically, Max Weber's theory of social stratification can be shown to be more appropriate in the analysis of socialist societies than those of Marx, on whose ideas the latter are supposed to be based. Max Weber's theory of social stratification is to be found in a few pages of *Wirtschaft und Gesellschaft*, (4th edition, Tubingen, 1956, II, pp. 531–40). There he argues that the basis of stratification is the distribution of power in a community. He defines power as 'the chances which a man or a group of men have to realise their will in a communal activity, even against the opposition of others taking part in it' (Runciman 1980, p. 43). He then goes on to argue that 'The distribution of power in a community is reflected in the existence of "classes", "status groups" and parties' (ibid.).

Weber's well-known definition of class is, according to him, appropriate

when (i) a large number of men have in common a specific causal factor influencing their chances in life, insofar as (ii) this factor has to do only with the possession of economic goods and the interests involved in earning a living, and furthermore (iii) in the conditions of the market in commodities or labour. (ibid.)

In Yugoslavia most of the means of production were taken into 'social ownership' in 1944. The principle of their self-management by entire workforces in individual enterprises was introduced in 1949. Much of the old urban apartment stock was also turned over to self-management by local interest communities in the 1970s. From the end of the Second World War until the 1990s the major and large-scale means of production and reproduction have been in 'social ownership' in Yugoslavia. Thus, the possession of economic goods has not been determined by market conditions and it is incorrect to describe different social groups in such societies as social classes, at least in the context of Weber's definition of them.

Nevertheless, social ownership has not removed all forms of social stratification, nor has it automatically created an egalitarian society. 'The trouble is that there is no clear definition of social ownership. In practice such assets are owned by the state as society's agent' (Lydall 1989, p. 94). Conflicts over the use and distribution of assets therefore focus on the state and the queues that it manages which replace markets for the allocation of scarce resources.

According to Weber, '"Classes" are formed in accordance with relations of production and acquisition of wealth, while "status groups" are formed according to the principles *governing* [emphasis added] their consumption of goods in the context of specific "life-styles"' (Runciman 1980, p. 54). We argue here that the substitution of government-managed queues for markets in socialist societies is therefore the basis for the replacement of a system of social stratification in which social classes are the major groups with one where 'status situation' is the major distinguishing feature between groups in conflict.

'"Status situation" . . . refer[s] to all those typical components of people's destinies which are determined by a specific social evaluation of "status", whether positive or negative when that evaluation is based on some common characteristic shared by many people' (Runciman 1980, p. 48). According to Weber the 'normal' origin of almost all social status is 'usurpation'. Djilas (1985) has described the process of usurpation in Yugoslavia:

As soon as the partisans entered Belgrade, Tito selected for himself a fine royal palace in Dedinje (Belgrade), a villa, hunting preserves, and various estates. He also took over the royal train. All the other leaders from the federal level down to the lowest district level, followed his example. A new ruling class materialized, 'spontaneously and systematically'. (Lydall 1989, p. 214)

According to Weber's concept this 'ruling class' should properly be defined as a status group. Its formation is clearly based on usurpation and its continuation is not based on market conditions.

Until 1990, when the Communist party was defeated in free elections held in the republics of Croatia and Slovenia, several Yugoslav status groups could be distinguished in descending order from the ruling Communist party members. The main status groups in 'self-management enterprise[s] resolve themselves primarily into 3, the Party, the managers and the workers' (Lydall 1984, p. 113). Other status groups that can be distinguished according to the level and type of their education are technical experts, intellectuals and peasants (ibid., p. 215).

Weber's concept of social stratification is appropriate to the analysis of socialist societies not only because of their development of status groups but also because of the significance of the party in both Weberian theory and those societies. He summarises the place of classes, status groups and parties in systems of social stratification as follows:

'Classes' are properly at home in the economic order, 'status groups' in the social order, that is, in the sphere of *distribution* [emphasis added] of status . . . Parties . . . are primarily at home in the sphere of power. There activity is concerned with social power, that is, with exerting influence on communal action, whatever its form. (Runciman 1980, p. 55)

Communal action is of great importance to parties. It has, until 1990 at least, also provided a crucial distinction between the activities of parties in socialist and capitalist societies. In socialist societies communist parties have not sought to exert influence over communal action but rather to *dominate* it (another key Weberian concept):

Communal action by parties, as opposed to classes or status groups, always requires the forming of an association. For it is always directed towards a goal which is pursued in accordance with a plan: the goal may be an 'objective' one, in the sense of the fulfilment of some programme for ideal or material ends, or it may be a 'personal' goal, in the sense of sinecures, power and, as a consequence, status for the leader and members, or, and indeed usually, all these things at once. Such activity is therefore only possible within a community, which, for its part, is in some way or other constituted as an association, that is, possesses some form of rational organization and an apparatus of personnel which is ready to bring about the goals in question. For the whole aim of parties is to influence such an apparatus and, wherever possible, to ensure that it is made up of party members. (Runciman 1980, p. 55)

This Weberian analysis of the role of parties describes almost exactly the League of Communists of Yugoslavia (SKJ).

Finally, Marx's belief that an historical progression from classical through feudal and capitalist societies to socialism is completely misplaced. A somewhat academic joke, current in Slovenian circles, is that 'communism is only an intermediate stage between capitalism and capitalism.' The recent upheavals in virtually the whole of Eastern Europe all seem to point in this direction.

Recent experiences throughout Eastern Europe show that the Marxist socialist experiment has been a failure and is drawing to a close. If it is indeed replaced with contemporary forms of capitalism, this calls into question Marx's interpretation of history and his evaluation of the causal connections between economy and historical change. If we are able to see, with the benefit of hindsight, the transient nature of communist/socialist regimes, then it will be necessary to reinterpret the causes of the directions of contemporary historical change.

Theoretical issues such as these lie at the heart of the *raison d'être* for studying Eastern Europe. The general conclusion that we draw here is that in many respects the work of Max Weber forms a more productive starting-point for understanding the nature of communist societies than does that of Marx, on which they are supposed to be based.

Economic, social and ideological constraints

After the Second World War Yugoslavia was confronted by a range of economic, social and ideological constraints. Some of these were unique to the country and some were commonly found among other East European states. But as with all the newly formed communist regimes, in no country did they start with a *tabula rasa*.

Among the common constraints, those of the economy were among the most significant. The choices facing Yugoslavia were limited to three basic alternatives. These were to

1. remain primarily an agricultural economy producing raw materials for internal consumption and export;
2. gradually develop a mixed economy and selected exports;
3. adopt a national plan to become an industrialised economy.

At the time it was thought by many underdeveloped economies that national industrialisation was the most efficacious course of action. It was also thought that single parties might be the driving-force that could achieve this objective.

While this may have been true in some circumstances, Communist party adoption of key Marxist economic concepts has frustrated adequate achievements in practice. In particular, the socialisation of the means of production has not produced the intended results or sufficient industrialisation and economic growth. The net result has been a massive failure of the economic system to match expectations and aspirations with achievements.

One of the main reasons for this is the inability of communism to change persistent individual behavioural characteristics. In particular, it does not offer decentralised incentives to support the objectives of the economic system. This means that people adapt to the system of necessity but often subvert its institutions in practice. This allows the people rather than the system itself to survive. They have achieved this by creating a substantial 'grey' market economy amounting to some 30–40 per cent of total gross domestic product. One contradiction that does persist in these circumstances is that although dissatisfaction with socialised production is widespread and privatisation is seen as the way forward, expectations that the state will continue to provide both employment and collective consumption remain. Such expectations seem destined to be disappointed.

A final major ideological contraint on Yugoslavia, and other East European states, is the continued existence and re-emergence of nationalism. No future government can ignore the nationalist issue. For a time, communist parties were able to displace the nationalist with the social class issue. Relaxation of the uncompromising domination of civil society has allowed old nationalist causes to be expressed in political action. This is something which our predominantly Slovene writers have not addressed. Nevertheless, it remains a serious and intractable problem for all the Yugoslav republics and even more so in the Soviet Union.

To some extent the decentralisation exemplified by self-management was intended to bypass the nationalist issue. It gave considerable significance and autonomy to individual republics. The strength of this autonomy has been such as to create something approaching regional autarchy both at the level of republican governments and in major enterprises. Thus, in order to placate the aspirations of individual republics the federal government has gone so far as to create unintentionally a confederation rather than a federation of separate republics. Even this threatens to fall apart with the diminution of single-party domination.

The limits of the Yugoslav experiment

Despite the fact that communist regimes are usually created by military force acting in the name of an ideological political will, in Europe at least, their continued existence appears to depend more on their ability to manage the economy and generate growth than on political ideology. In this respect they are remarkably like their Western counterparts. For this reason we reverse the order of our earlier discussions here and start with an evaluation of economic limitations.

Economy

In Part III Jože Mencinger and Bogomir Kovač showed how economic problems have driven political reforms and how the limits of Marxist adaptations to inadequate economic performance have been reached.

Jože Mencinger argued that two key elements of market economies were rejected when the system of contractual socialism was established. These were first, markets as basic mechanisms for resource allocation, and second, macro-economic policy and indicative planning as a means of indirectly regulating economic activities. Instead, social contracts, self-management agreements and social planning were adopted. Because this system was ideologically inspired it sought to ignore the 'laws' of economics and was operated by too many institutions. The result was poor economic performance. Between 1960 and 1980 the Yugoslav economy grew by only 70 per cent of the corresponding increases in Southern European market economies. Growth stagnated in the 1980s. Even 'official' unemployment rose to 16 per cent. Hyperinflation had set in by 1989.

Most East European economies were suffering from one or more of these major economic problems by the end of the 1980s. The socialist state apparatus could do little about them within its self-imposed ideological constraints. Apart from the political, military and economic élites, very few citizens of these countries could experience much in the way of material benefits after at least a generation of the socialist experiment. This proved to be a powerful stimulus to various types of mass social movement which eventually formed the basis of political protests. In Yugoslavia, poor economic performance, as much as anything else, led to the reform programme launched in 1988. Its objectives were no less than to create new, integral product, labour and capital markets. As Jože Mencinger pointed out, these are incompatible with social property and self-management.

Another major limitation for would-be socialist economies was encountered earlier in Yugoslavia than other East European states. It is that individual economies cannot be isolated indefinitely from the global world economy. The attempt to follow the example of the Soviet Union in using 'heavy industrial complexes' as the major method of rapid industrialisation has not been successful. The Yugoslav economy could not support such major complexes in every republic. Yet what one republic obtained all the others demanded. It has not proved possible to absorb all the products of these complexes internally or to export them profitably abroad. They have not usually been competitive in world markets.

Partly by choice and partly by force of circumstances, the Yugoslav economy has been disciplined and limited by conditions in the world economy. These conditions have included growth conditions, world markets and interest rates. As world economic growth slowed down in the 1970s and 1980s, so the actual and potential demand for Yugoslavian labour and products also declined. This left overproduced industrial materials with inadequate demand at home and declining markets abroad. Interest rate policies operated by the federal government and Yugoslav banks were extraordinarily unrealistic. No economy can continue to operate like this indefinitely. This proved to be the case in Yugoslavia.

A further limitation of the Yugoslav experiment has been that continuing conflicts between capital and labour have not been resolved by concentrating on democracy in production and at the local territorial level. In conditions of socially owned means of production, capital has no specific private or public owners. As a consequence, investment decisions are deformed by the lack of representation of the 'interests of capital' and the unitary interests of employed labour to extract higher wages from production processes. In the past this has often been temporarily achieved at the direct expense of reinvestment or inefficient capital intensification. Much of this has been supported by the banks at subsidised interest rates and based on political rather than economic criteria.

Conflicts between the need for efficient capital investment and the needs of labour have bedevilled other East European economies, most spectacularly in Poland. One of the lessons emerging for most of them is that the needs of labour cannot be met without economic growth. Economic growth is not optimised by centralised and inefficient capital investment decisions. Indeed, the latter can be so poor that growth turns to decline and the needs of labour are decreasingly satisfied. Recent economic history in the Soviet Union is an example of this problem.

Polity

Although the problems of economic growth are at the heart of all government activities, they are also inextricably bound up with politics. The main reason for this in Western democracies is the question of how the fruits of economic growth are distributed between different organisations and groups. This is a key political issue at all levels of government.

East European states have been limited by the additional problems of politically dominated economic systems and the ideological expectation that labour should do better in distributional conflicts in communist than in capitalist systems. In practice, the benefits accruing to labour in the former systems have been limited by the false assumption that they would axiomatically be better off once private economic property had been abolished. As a result of this assumption, distributional issues were officially excluded from public debate and overt political action. This did not prevent them arising. All communist systems, however, have been ideologically and politically limited in their ability to handle them satisfactorily.

In Yugoslavia, the early attempts to develop elements of a self-managed market economy in the helpful context of world economic growth, soon challenged the monopolistic position of the Communist party. Important decisions could be taken by firms and workers without reference to the party and the state. While this could be seen as a 'withering' of state functions, it subverted the leading role of the party, which has never shown much enthusiasm for withering away and losing the privileges enjoyed by its individual members. The 1974 constitutional reforms and the 1976 Associated Labour Act established the system of self-management as it existed until the end of the 1980s, but their main function was to reinstate the Communist party at the heart of all significant decisions.

Janez Šmidovnik analysed the problems of self-management during this period in its three main institutional settings. These were in enterprises, communes and public services.

He argued that the self-management of enterprises has suffered from four main problems. First, there was the problem of ownership. The Marxist assumption that revolutionary changes in economic property ownership would axiomatically benefit economic performance and labour has proved to be naïvely optimistic. In practice the private ownership of economic property was transformed into a system in which neither institutions nor individuals took up all the rights and responsibilities of ownership. The consequence was that the performance of Yugoslav enterprises was limited by the fact that they had no real owners of any kind concerned with efficient capital investment.

The second problem followed from the first. Where the state, directors and workers in enterprises did not accept ownership responsibilities, there was an inclination for them to use the enterprise for their own ends. The state as represented by the Communist party intervened continually in attempts to maintain some progress towards its utopian objectives. Directors represented a political stronghold in the enterprise, and while following party instructions, also tended to aim mainly for a 'quiet life'. Workers proved to have little interest or ability to manage firms. Their main aim was to obtain the highest possible wages compatible with the least responsibility for decision-making. This severely limited the inclination or ability of enterprises either to generate much in the way of internal investment or to use external funding efficiently.

The third problem was that under this system it was very difficult to make authoritative decisions in the light of any independent economic or managerial assessment of what they should be for any particular enterprise *per se*. The result is that large parts of the Yugoslav and other East European economies are actually running at a loss. Despite the strictures of Marxist theory, this is not a state of affairs that can continue indefinitely.

The fourth problem identified by Janez Šmidovnik is the attempt to solve economic and social problems mainly within the political and organisational confines of the commune. This is both the basic political and economic cell in the Yugoslav political economy. It has ensured both the geographic fragmentation of enterprises and constant state intervention in them. It could be compared to the unthinkable possibility that Western local authorities should dominate the business decisions of firms operating within their particular areas.

Janez Šmidovnik also turns a critical eye on the provision of public services. This might have been expected to be one of the major concerns and strengths of a communist regime. In reality it emerges as another limited element of their performance. Influenced by Marxist doctrine on the withering away of the state, public services were supposed to be provided by voluntary co-operation between those who could provide them and those who needed them. In theory this excluded the necessity of state intervention.

The institutional vehicles for achieving these ends were self-management interest communities. They were introduced between 1970 and 1980. They were supposed to provide the vehicles for a 'free exchange of labour' between suppliers and consumers, who would negotiate between themselves on exactly what was needed. The money to pay for public services was by 'voluntary' contributions made by enterprises and also deducted from wages. One of the main limits of this system was that in the poorer communes enterprises and workers were often unable to make adequate contributions for the provision of their own services. A surprising limitation of such a socialist system was that even the republics have not installed mechanisms for making progressive redistributions from richer to poorer communes for the provision of public services.

In addition to these difficulties, communes have also been expected to play a role in activities more often associated with central governments in the West. They have therefore been overloaded with functions. Paradoxically this attempt to pile responsibilities on to the communes has led, among other things, to the re-emergence of local communities which are not dissimilar in size and function to the old 'parishes' which the new communes were supposed to supersede.

The Yugoslav system of communes also raises the paradox that such a system only seems possible if it is established from above by a unitary if not totalitarian state. That being so, there has always been a question mark over the limits of power exercised, particularly between the communes and republics. This grey area has led to portrayals of their power relationships as two pyramids configured like an 'X'. It is clear that power resides at both the top and the grass-roots of the system. It is not clear how conflicts between republics and communes are resolved around the intersection.

Zagorka Golubović argues that there is in any case a major limitation on the ability of one-party communist states to develop real self-government. They simply do not have the major prerequisite for such a development. This is a developed civil society separate and independent from the state. Communist regimes have prevented such developments because they are rightly seen as posing challenges to the unfettered domination of all aspects of life by the party. Although the idea of self-management implies such a division in Western thought, in Yugoslavia it has proved to be a device to legitimise the continuing domination of the Communist party behind a façade of apparently decentralised and democratic decision-making. However, as Zagorka Golubović says, the real power structure remained the same.

A key test of where the limits of the power of ordinary citizens lie is the distributional outcomes of economic and political decisions. We showed, in Part IV, that inequalities in social security and services have been maintained under self-management. Barbara Verlič-Dekleva addressed the phenomenon of the overlap between economic and social policy. She pointed out that although human and social equality were major objectives of the post-war transformation of Yugoslavia, they have not been achieved in practice. Yugoslav social policy has not been a means to reduce social inequalities. After nearly half a century of the communist experiment major inequalities persist between regions, workers, those without work and those confined to the 'grey' economy.

Pavel Gantar and Srna Mandič examined the effects of communist housing policies and their contribution to social equality. Shortages in housing supply have persisted. The formal construction sector is unable to supply enough housing. Workers have therefore been left to build their own accommodation. A large, informal self-build sector has developed in most major cities. Major housing inequalities have therefore emerged between those in the more desirable social housing and those in self-build accommodation.

In urban areas as a whole, Ognjen Čaldarović showed that inequalities in location have been added to those of housing quality to produce further social inequality in cities. He showed that different social status groups were in possession of different housing rights, and that in Zagreb higher social status groups were found concentrated disproportionately in central areas while workers were more often concentrated on the periphery.

All this evidence shows how limited the progressive redistribution of collective consumption goods and services has been in Yugoslavia. The advantage of conducting such an analysis in that country is that more public empirical evidence is available there than in most other communist/socialist regimes. It seems probable, however, that the findings would be repeated elsewhere if the data were published.

In order to change the political agenda on such issues, Tomaž Mastnak argued that it is essential to separate the state and government from the party and to introduce a pluralist party system. In fact in 1990 free elections took place in both Croatia and Slovenia for the first time since the Second World War. It is doubtful if this would have been the case without the prior existence of New Social Movements. There is no evidence that the Communist party will relinquish power or the state wither away without the intervention of such human agents. The continuing conflicts between these two republics and communist-dominated Serbia only serve to demonstrate the limits of peaceful democratic reform in such regimes.

Ultimately it seems highly unlikely that real decentralisation can exist in a single-party state. Despite decentralisation to communes using systems of self-management in Yugoslavia, the ubiquitous presence of the Communist party at all levels and in all parts of this system meant that in reality republican party control could be exercised at all levels of government. Self-management has not meant autonomous self-government.

Lessons for the future of Yugoslavia

Our foreward by Živko Pregl, vice-president of the Federal Executive Council of the Socialist Federal Republic of Yugoslavia, argues that Yugoslavia has embarked on an ambitious programme of reforms. Democratic elections have already been held in two of the republics. Changes are taking place. In this final section we note some of the intractable issues that effective change must confront.

The first of these is the technical problem of privatisation. Our authors have shown this to be a complex and lengthy process. The translation of social ownership into legal forms where the actual owners are identifiable and their responsibilities clear cannot be achieved overnight. There is a lack of indigenous entrepreneurs, market-oriented and trained managers, capital markets and a commercial banking system.

Bogomir Kovač examined the problem of turning a Basic Organisation of Associated Labour into a capitalist, market organisation. In the contractual socialist system business decisions were made by a triumvirate of workers' councils, managers and the state. Business policy was therefore quite different from that of market firms. Losses were covered by the banks! Accounting and budgetary procedures were extremely 'soft'.

Proposals for reform have included tighter financial controls and entrepreneurial development. Both pose major technical difficulties. In the first place there is the serious problem of putting a realistic value or price on a firm without the operation of an existing capital market. This means that Western accountants would find it extremely difficult to decide how much capital a firm was employing, and therefore whether it was making a profit or not.

In the second place, it is difficult to privatise a firm without some idea of what it is worth. Four different strategies have been adopted in Yugoslavia to overcome this problem. One technique has been to establish holding companies. The resources of Basic Organisations of Associated Labour are put into such companies and one of their main tasks is to convert their finances on to a 'normal' accounting basis. Another technique has been to distribute shares to workers on the basis of their past contributions to the Association. This is complex and does not necessarily mean that they can then be sold to other buyers. A third device involves selling shares to managers and workers. This also raises the question of how to arrive at an initial price for those shares. Finally, some sales have been made to newly formed 'democratic' financial institutions. These include pension funds and the emerging insurance sector.

Similar technical problems confront economists, governments and firms all over Eastern Europe. It is just impossible to translate collective economic property into limited liability companies overnight. Many Eastern economists believe that this process will take at least a decade. The problem that this raises for many states is that, although it has been possible to change institutions almost overnight, it will take much longer to transform collective into market economies. Citizens' expectations of quick economic payoffs as a result of political change seem destined to be disappointed. The difficult question for Yugoslavia and other countries is how long such expectations can remain unmet without generating pressures for further political change.

Another thorny issue for the future is that of foreign ownership. This was a major pre-war issue when much of the Yugoslav economy was owned by Austrians and Germans. There is a presumption against too much foreign ownership but the establishment of completely free markets will make this difficult to moderate. It will not be helped by the lack of Yugoslav personnel, institutions and capital.

Most East European economies face the possibility of becoming Third World-type locations for West European firms. The attraction of cheap and relatively skilled labour combined with fewer development regulations could lead to the 'colonisation' of the East by the West. Measures to prevent such an eventuality should include the requirement for 'local' participation in all ventures; full technology transfer; and perhaps slower growth than could have been the case with full-scale branch plant colonisation.

Finally, there is no guarantee that the introduction of markets will actually improve the performance of the Yugoslav economy. Depending on their exposure to foreign competition, many inefficient enterprises may have to close. The inevitable result will be greater official unemployment. Worker tolerance of this is likely to be limited and could be another factor leading to further political difficulties.

The second major lesson of history is that throughout Eastern Europe social inequalities have persisted under communist regimes. New ones have been added. Thus, one thing that the abolition of private ownership of the means of production did not do, was to create automatically greater social equality. This has been one of the reasons for the declining support of communist systems. On the other hand, free market economies tend to increase rather than decrease social inequalities. Their adoption to improve economic performance will therefore require state interventions to redistribute some of the resulting benefits in order to maintain political support for them.

Change in Yugoslavia must therefore confront the familiar Western issue of the conflict between profit maximisation and social investment. Both are required to maintain and legitimate the system but neither can be maximised simultaneously. Although this conflict lies at the heart of Marxist theory, regimes based on Marx's solutions have not resolved it. There are few long-term international examples to draw on where this major conflict has been resolved. They are mostly to be found in comparatively homogeneous North European Scandinavian countries.

The third issue affecting most East European states is whether the entire, socialist paradigm is really being abandoned, and, if so, how to disentangle the economy, the polity and society from each other and the all-embracing control of a single party. There is some doubt and suspicion in many states about whether Communist party members will really abandon their cherished power and privileges. From being in the vanguard of change, Yugoslavia has been overtaken by other East European countries for this very reason. So far the Serbian Communist party has shown no signs of relinquishing republican or federal power. Its domination of the national army puts it in a strong position to resist major change and the breakup of the federation.

In Western Europe democratic institutions have evolved over long periods of time. Although there are continuing arguments about their true separation, compared with Eastern Europe, they are relatively autonomous from each other. However, the resulting mixed economies, welfare states and a significant middle social class were not put in place overnight. The institutional structures in place in East and West Europe are now very different from one another. It remains to be seen whether those in the West can be used as instant models to be aspired to in the East.

Despite all these caveats and reservations, these are nevertheless exciting times in which to live in Eastern Europe. The deprivations of a generation will not be remedied overnight. Nevertheless significant change is now a possibility which could not even be imagined realistically only a year or so ago.

References

Lydall, H., 1984. *Yugoslav Socialism: Theory and Practice*, Oxford, Clarendon Press.

—— H., 1989. *Yugoslavia in Crisis*, Oxford, Clarendon Press.

McFarlane, B., 1988. *Yugoslavia: politics, economics and society*, London, Pinter.

Runciman, W. G., 1980. *Max Weber: Selections in Translation*, Cambridge, Cambridge University Press.

NAMES INDEX

SUBJECT INDEX